Awesome Experiments in
Electricity
&Magnetism

Michael DiSpezio

Illustrations by Catherine Leary

Sterling Publishing Co., Inc
New York

ACKNOWLEDGMENTS

Again, I have had the wonderful opportunity to work with my Sterling team on this brand-new series of science books. I'd like to acknowledge the dedication and ability of my energetic and always upbeat editor, Hazel Chan, and the talent and kid-friend style of artist Catherine Leary. I'd also like to recognize Sheila Barry for nurturing and encouraging this series from its conception.

In addition, there are many instructors, colleagues, and friends who have unselfishly shared their expertise and wide-ranging experiences acquired in the "trenches" of science education. It is their thoughts, conceptualizations, explanations, and passion that continually sculpt my teaching style, writing, and philosophy.

I'd also like to thank my son, Anthony, for helping me tweak these experiments and continually see the world through the eyes of a child!

Library of Congress Cataloging-in-Publication Data

Dispezio, Michael A.
    Awesome experiments in electricity & magnetism / by Michael
Dispezio ; illustrated by Catherine Leary.
       p.   cm.
    Includes index.
    Summary: Provides instructions for over fifty experiments
demonstrating the properties of electricity and magnetism.
    ISBN 0-8069-9819-9
    1. Electricity—Experiments—Juvenile literature. 2. Magnetism—Experiments—
Juvenile literature. [1. Electricity—Experiments. 2. Magnetism—
Experiments. 3. Experiments.] I. Leary, Catherine, ill. II. Title. III. Title: Awesome
experiments in electricity and magnetism.
QC529.2.D575   1998
537´.078—dc21   98-22439
                                         CIP
                                         AC

10 9 8 7 6 5 4 3 2 1

First paperback edition published in 2000 by
Sterling Publishing Company, Inc.
387 Park Avenue South, New York, N.Y. 10016
© 1998 by Michael A. DiSpezio
Distributed in Canada by Sterling Publishing
c/o Canadian Manda Group, One Atlantic Avenue, Suite 105
Toronto, Ontario, Canada M6K 3E7
Distributed in Great Britain and Europe by Chris Lloyd
463 Ashley Road, Parkstone, Poole, Dorset, BH14 0AX, England
Distributed in Australia by Capricorn Link (Australia) Pty Ltd.
P.O. Box 6651, Baulkham Hills, Business Centre, NSW 2153, Australia
Manufactured in the United States of America
All rights reserved

Sterling ISBN 0-8069-9819-9 Trade
                0-8069-9820-2 Paper

C O N T E N T S

PART ONE
STATIC ELECTRICITY

PART TWO
CURRENT ELECTRICITY

PART THREE
MAGNETS AND MAGNETISM

SAFETY FIRST

Follow all instructions, cautions, and safety notes. To protect your eyes, wear safety goggles when performing all of the experiments. Conduct every experiment with proper supervision. Have an adult perform all steps that use a flame, wall outlet, sharp point, cutting edge, or any other potentially dangerous tool. Neither the author nor the publisher shall be liable for injuries that may be caused by not following the experiment steps or adhering to the safety notes.

INTRODUCTION

This book is a guide. Its primary purpose is to accompany you through more than seventy adventures in learning. As you perform these experiments, you'll celebrate the magic of science. You'll also observe how science isn't a distant notion limited to classrooms, laboratories, books, and PBS specials. Science is all around you!

Unlike many other subjects, science is constructed from inquiry. This philosophy of exploration is a cornerstone of the National Science Education Standards. It is also the premise upon which the *Awesome Experiments in Science* series has been created. With an increased focus on understanding (and NOT memorizing facts), these books offer kid-friendly experiments that will engage, harness, and nurture your thinking skills.

PART ONE

STATIC ELECTRICITY

1.1 ALL CHARGED UP

*W*hen you hear the word "electricity," what do you think of? Most of us imagine a flow of energy along wires that lights bulbs, spins motors, and rings bells. This type of moving energy is called current electricity. But there's another type of electricity that behaves differently than this flowing form. It's called static electricity.

The dictionary defines the word "static" as stationary or non-moving. In other words, when something is static it stays put. This first experiment will introduce you to this fun and non-flowing form of electricity.

Materials
* two balloons
* a piece of wool or felt
* tape
* 1-foot thread

To Do
Inflate two balloons. Attach a 1-foot length of thread to each of the balloons. Use tape to attach the thread of one balloon to the bottom of a desk (or the roof of a favorite hideout).

Rub the hanging balloon with a piece of wool or felt. You should give it at least twenty back-and-forth rubs. Release this balloon and let it hang.

Rub the second balloon with the wool or felt. Hold it by the end of the thread and bring it near the first balloon. What happens to the balloons? Tape the second balloon close enough to the first so that they appear to be flying away from each other.

The Science
Most objects start off with a neutral charge. When they are rubbed with certain materials, however, they can take on a positive or negative charge.

As a balloon was rubbed with the wool, invisible negative charges flowed from the wool onto the balloon. As a result, the balloon's charge balance was destroyed. The extra charges gave the balloon a net negative charge. Once transferred, the tiny charges stayed put (hence the "static" in static electricity).

At a distance, the two charged balloons did not have enough charge to affect each other. When they got closer, however, things changed. Since both balloons had a negative charge, they repelled each other. This force caused them to fling out and remain apart.

CHECK IT OUT! Suppose a third charged balloon was brought near these two. What shape would the repelling balloons form?

1.2 POSITIVE CONTACT

*F*rom the previous experiment, we made negative charges transfer onto a balloon when it was rubbed with wool. Because the balloon now has more negative charges than positive charges, it has a net negative charge. This type of "charging" is called *contact charging.*

Contact charging can also produce objects with a positive charge. For an object to become positive, it must lose some of its negative charges. This loss offsets the neutral balance to produce a net positive charge.

Materials

* *10-inch strip of nylon fabric (if needed, cut the nylon from a stocking)*
* *a pair of scissors*
* *plastic grocery bag*

To Do

Use your scissors to cut a 10-inch strip of nylon. Firmly hold the middle of the strip, allowing the halves to hang downward. Grasp the nylon with the plastic bag. Stroke both halves of the fabric several times. What happens when you stop stroking the nylon? What causes the nylon to behave this way?

The Science

Unlike wool, your plastic does not easily give up its negative charges. On the contrary, it has a tendency to take in negative charges. When the plastic rubbed along the nylon, negative charges transferred to the plastic material. This left the nylon strips with a positive charge. Since both both hanging halves had the same charge, they repelled each other, causing the free ends to separate.

CHECK IT OUT! Can you charge a plastic bag by rubbing it with wool?

1.3 MAIN ATTRACTION

So far, you've observed what happens when objects of the same charge are brought together. The negative balloons repel each other. The positive nylon strips repel each other. But what happens when a negative balloon and a positive strip are brought near each other?

Materials

* *nylon strip*
* *1-foot thread*
* *tape*
* *balloon*
* *wool*
* *plastic grocery bag*

To Do

Attach a 1-foot length of thread to an inflated balloon. Charge the balloon by rubbing it with wool. Use tape to attach the thread to the edge of a table or desk.

Charge the nylon strip by rubbing it with a plastic bag. Stroke the strip several times to ensure that it becomes sufficiently charged. Bring the strip near the hanging balloon. What happens?

Release the strip. Does it stick to the balloon or is it repelled by this oppositely-charged object?

The Science

Like charges repel. Unlike charges attract.

Both the balloon and strip were charged by contact charging. The balloon took on a net negative charge. The nylon strip took on a net positive charge.

When the negative and positive charges were close enough, the objects moved together. At close range, the attraction was strong enough to stick the nylon to the balloon's surface.

CHECK IT OUT! Can rubbing with nylon or paper towel produce contact charging?

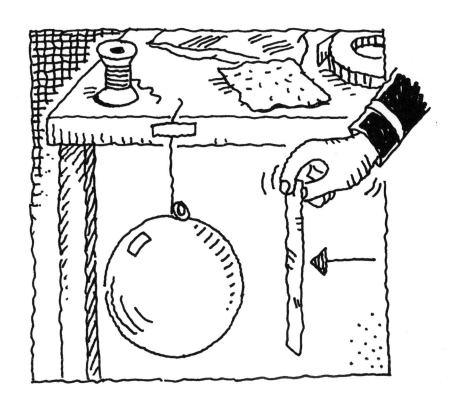

1.4 STATIC GLUE

*B*irthday parties occur throughout the year. Most likely, some of the parties you've attended had balloon decorations. By rubbing the balloons and placing them against the wall, they would magically cling to the dry flat surface. Why?

Materials
* *balloon*
* *a piece of wool or felt*

To Do
Inflate a balloon and stroke it with a piece of wool or felt. If you don't have any fabric material, you can stroke the balloon against your hair. Place the balloon against the wall. What happens? How long will the balloon cling to the wall? Recharge the balloon and observe how well it clings to other objects, such as wood, a metal cabinet, and glass.

The Science
As the balloon is rubbed with wool, it becomes negatively charged. This charge produces an invisible electric field.

When the balloon is brought close to the wall, the negative charges in the wall are repelled by the balloon's negative field. These charges move deeper (migrate) into the wall. As they leave the wall region nearest the balloon, they create a positive wall surface. As a result, the positive wall and the negative balloon attract.

The wall became charged by *induction*. In this type of charging, objects don't touch. Instead, an electric field causes charges to migrate in surrounding materials. Although the number of charges remain the same, they are unequally distributed. Regions with more positive charges take on a net positive charge. Regions with more negative charges take on a net negative charge.

CHECK IT OUT! Can you charge up a balloon if you alternate the direction of the strokes?

1.5 CHARGE IT ON PLASTIC

*H*ave you ever sat on a plastic lawn chair and placed your bare arms on the chair's surface? If so, you may have felt a "clinging" force sticking to your tiny arm hairs. This force is produced by the charged chair plastic. As your body shifted in the chair, electrons were transferred to the plastic material to produce a "sticky" sensation.

Materials

* *two 2 inch × 10 inch strips of plastic (cut from an overhead transparency or report cover)*
* *paper*
* *pair of scissors*

To Do

Use the scissors to cut two separate strips of plastic. The strips should be about 2 inches wide × 10 inches long. Place the strips side-by-side on a sheet of plain white paper.

Press your fingers down on the strip. Stroke both strips about ten times.

Pick up the strips by their edges and hold them together so that they can fall freely. What do you notice about the plastic strips? Do they fall freely or is there an invisible force at work?

The Science

As your fingers rubbed along the plastic, electrons were transferred. This produced a net charge in the plastic. Since both hanging strips had the same charge, they repelled each other and flew apart.

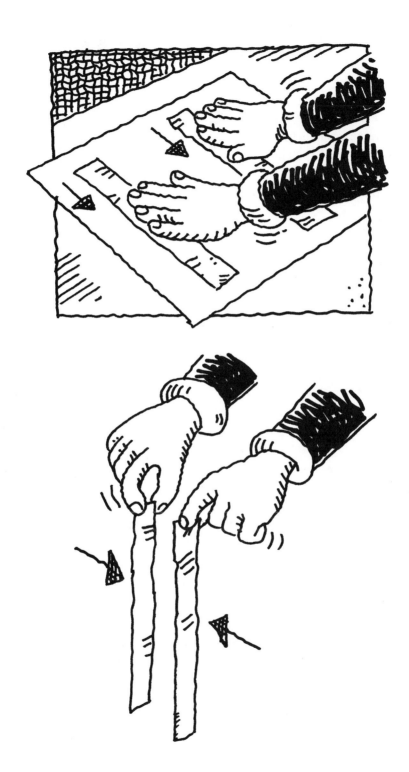

1.6 GHOST LEGS

The magician covers a box with a silk scarf. Slowly, she raises the box into the air. While holding the covered box, she suddenly flicks her wrist. The scarf goes limp and the box disappears. How did she do it? We're not telling, but we do have a magical activity that also produces a phantom shape in thin air.

Materials
* *sheer nylon stocking*
* *plastic grocery bag*
* *smooth wall*

To Do
With one hand, hold the top of the stocking against a flat wall. Use the other hand to stroke the stocking in one direction with the plastic grocery bag. As you stroke the nylon material, smooth it against the wall's surface.

After several strokes, release the stocking. What happens to the material? How is this similar to sticking balloons to a wall? How is it different?

Now gently grasp the top of the stocking and move it away from the wall. Make sure that it does not touch anything (including yourself). Hold out the stocking. What happens to its shape? Can you explain your observation?

The Science
As the plastic bag moves over the nylon, it picks up negative charges. This produces a stocking with a net positive charge. This charged stocking acts like the negatively-charged balloon and induces an opposite charge in the nearby wall. The negative and positive charges attract and the stocking clings to the wall. When the stocking is pulled from the wall, it still retains its net positive charge. These charges, which are distributed throughout the stocking material, push away from each other. This causes the stocking to "expand" and take on the leg shape it was manufactured in.

1.7 CHARGE IT

Objects that have like charges repel.

Objects that have unlike charges attract.

But what happens when one object has a charge and the other one is neutral? Can you guess how these objects would react, based upon what you observed in the previous experiment?

Materials

* two balloons
* two 1-foot-long threads
* tape
* a piece of wool

To Do

Inflate two balloons. Tie a 1-foot section of thread to each. Position the balloons so that they hang side-by-side, separated by several inches of space. Hold one of the balloons and stroke it with wool. Once this balloon has been charged, gently let it fall back into place. As it moves into its original position, what happens to the nearby neutral balloon? Can you explain what caused this action?

The Science

The balloon that was stroked with wool picked up a net negative charge. This charge repelled the negative charges in the neighboring balloon. As those charges moved to other regions of the balloon material, the nearby area became positive in charge. Attraction between the negative balloon and positive region of the neighboring balloon brought these charged objects together.

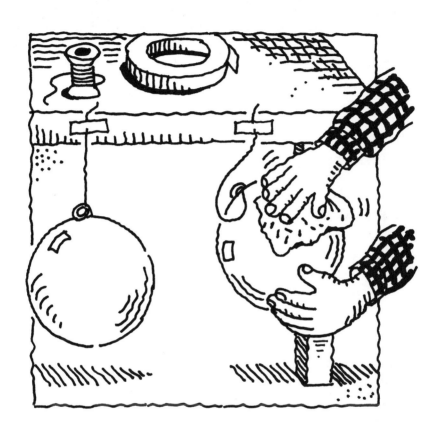

1.8 CHARGE THE COMB

On a dry, crisp day, find a totally quiet room. Comb your hair and listen carefully. Do you hear anything?

Materials
* *plastic comb*
* *paper*

To Do
Tear up a sheet of paper into small pieces. Place these pieces in a small pile on your desk.

Run a plastic comb through your hair several times. Then position the comb above the pile of paper. What happens?

The Science
Paper, like most materials, starts out with an equal and random distribution of negative and positive charges. Since the charges are equal in number, they cancel each other out so that the paper has a net neutral charge.

As the comb rubs against hair, negative charges are transferred onto the comb. Through *contact*, the comb takes on a net negative charge.

When the comb is placed above the paper, it exerts its negative field, which causes the negative charges in the paper to move away from the comb. These negative charges migrate through the paper and collect at the paper's far side. Through *induction*, the closer region becomes positive.

The attraction between this positive region of the paper and the negative comb is strong enough to overcome gravity. The paper pieces jump from the tabletop to the comb.

As the paper remains on the comb, the comb's negative charges migrate into the paper. This cancels the nearby charge and the paper falls to the tabletop.

CHECK IT OUT! Would pieces of aluminum foil or plastic wrap behavior like the paper?

1.9 BARREL ROLL

So far, you've learned that paper sticks well to both combs and walls. But did you know you can move a rolled-up piece of paper by static attraction? Here's how.

Materials
* *paper*
* *pair of scissors*
* *tape*
* *comb*
* *wool*

To Do
Cut out a strip of paper about 1 inch wide and 4 inches long. Roll the paper into a cylinder and secure its shape with a small section of tape. Charge up the comb by running it through your hair or stroking it with a piece of wool or flannel. Place the comb near the paper barrel. What happens?

The Science
Stroking the comb gives it a net negative charge. As it was brought near the neutral-charged paper barrel, it induced a charge in the paper. Negative charges on the closer side of the paper were repelled away, leaving a net positive region. This region was attracted to the comb. When inertia and friction were overcome, the paper rolled towards the comb.

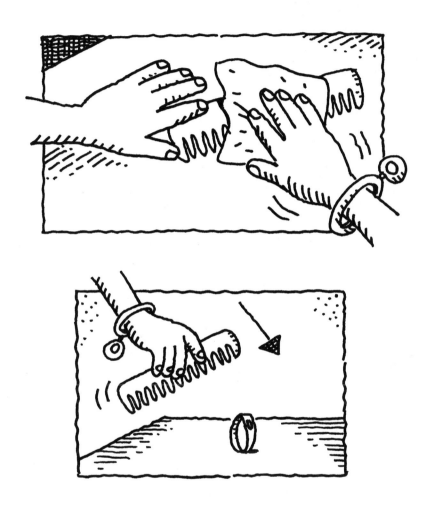

1.10 CRACKLES & POPS

"What's on TV tonight?"
"Arm hairs and paper scraps."

Materials

* *television set or computer monitor*
* *a sheet of paper*

To Do

Switch the television set on. Roll up your shirt sleeve. Place your fore-arm against the television screen. Hear anything? Feel anything? Slowly move your arm across the screen. What happens now?

Tear up a sheet of paper into small fingernail-sized pieces. Put these pieces on the television screen and take your hand away. Do the pieces fall to the floor? Slowly move your hand just above these pieces of paper. Do any of the pieces react? If so, how? Touch several of them. Does this change their behavior?

The Science

The television screen is a charged surface. As your arm moved along the screen, it entered the screen's electric field. This field induced a charge on your arm hairs so that they became attracted to the screen. As a result, you felt them standing on end! As the hairs approached the screen, the static charge produced a small jump of electricity that made a crackling sound.

Like your arm hairs, the pieces of paper became charged by the screen's electric field. The paper's charge caused it to stick to the screen. When your hand moved above the paper, the charges shifted again to cause the paper to fly off the screen.

CHECK IT OUT! Why does a layer of dust also seem to form on a television screen?

1.11 ROUND THE BEND

"*N*ever use an electric appliance while you are in the bathtub!"

Although it is not a great conductor of electricity, water can easily conduct the current that flows from your home's power outlet. The results are often deadly.

What about static electricity? Can water interact with non-moving charges?

Materials
* *plastic comb*
* *pencil*
* *plastic pen*
* *a piece of wool*
* *sink*

To Do
Turn on a water faucet. Adjust the flow to a slow but steady stream.

Pass the plastic comb through your hair several times. Slowly bring the comb close to the water. What happens?

Stroke a plastic pen with a piece of wool material. Now bring the pen towards the water. What happens?

Repeat this activity using a pencil. Does the pencil produce the same effect as the pen? Why?

The Science
Plastic is a good material for storing electric charges. As the comb traveled through your hair, it picked up a negative charge. When it was brought close to the running water, it induced a positive charge in the closest part of the flow. The positive water and the negative comb attracted and produced a bend in the flow.

As you might have guessed, wool is a poor storage material for an electric charge. It did not keep enough charge to affect the water stream.

CHECK IT OUT! Could a bend in a water flow be produced by using plastic that had been rubbed with silk?

1.12 COMMANDING PERFORMANCE

"Come to me."

"Go that way. I command you."

"Turn in a circle."

Have you ever wished for a magic wand? You know the type. You can use it to command the movment of all sorts of objects. Well, in this activity, you'll have a chance to build this type of wand. The "magic," however, is hidden in the invisible field of electric charges.

Materials

* *table tennis ball*
* *plastic pen*
* *wool*

To Do

Set the table tennis ball on a flat surface. Steady it so that it doesn't move.

Stroke the plastic pen with the wool. After stroking the pen, move it close to the table tennis ball. What happens?

Try moving the pen so that the ball moves with a continuous motion. Can you do it?

The Science

As the pen was stroked with the wool, negative charges were transferred between the materials. These charges left the wool and accumulated on the pen. The pen became negatively charged.

When the negative pen was placed near the table tennis ball, its electric field affected the charges of the ball. The nearby negative charges were repelled by the pen and moved away. This left a relatively positive side of the ball. This positive side and the negative pen attracted. Once inertia and friction were overcome, the ball began moving.

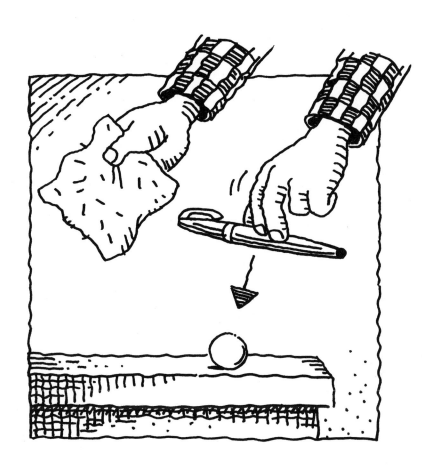

1.13 IT'S A WRAP

*H*ave you ever tried to cover a bowl with plastic wrapping, only to discover that the wrapping seemed to have a mind of its own? You placed it one way, and the wrapping seemed to fly out in the opposite direction. To further complicate things, the wrapping also seemed to have an uncanny attraction for both your hands. Although it might have been a frustrating experience, it can be used to teach real science.

Materials
* lightweight plastic food wrapping
* wooden ruler or wooden paint stirrer

To Do
Cut out a section of plastic wrapping that is about 20 inches long × 2 inches wide. Spread this strip out against a flat wall. As you rub the wrapping, press it out in all directions.

Once it clings to the wall, peel back the wrapping and hang it over a ruler. While holding the ruler with one hand, place your other hand into the space between the hanging plastic wrapping. What happens? Can you explain your observations?

The Science
As you pushed the plastic wrapping against the wall, charges were transferred. The plastic took on a net negative charge. As the strips hung near your hand, they induced a positive charge in your skin's surface. This positive charge was sufficient to attract the negative plastic wrapping and it automatically wrapped up your hand.

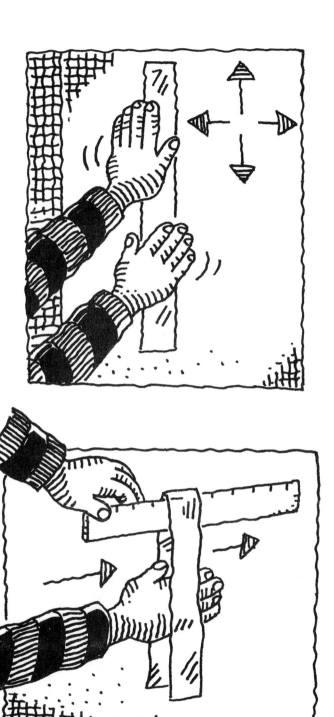

1.14 STAND UP AND BE COUNTED

E lectrical charges flow easily through metal. Yet we haven't used metal in any of the experiments. Why? Because the problem with using metal is that—unlike materials such as plastic, paper, and nylon—metal is *not* lightweight. It's heavy. Metal's mass can easily "mask" the attraction of electrostatic forces. But for those of you who still want a metal experiment, here's this stand-up activity.

Materials
* *a sheet of light-gauge aluminum foil*
* *pair of scissors*
* *clear plastic food bowl with cover*
* *wool*

To Do
Use your scissors to cut out several human-like figures from a sheet of light-gauge aluminum foil. The figures from head to toe should be slightly shorter than the depth of the plastic food bowl (from bottom to cover).

Place the figures in the bowl. Cover the bowl. Use the wool to vigorously stroke the bowl's cover. What happens?

The Science
As the plastic cover was stroked, it acquired a negative charge. This charge induced a positive charge in the near ends of the aluminum figures.

Since the heads were the lighter end of the cutouts, they probably were the first part that moved upwards. Since the charge wasn't great enough to overcome all of the figures' weight, they did not fly up and cling to the cover. Instead, the aluminum cutouts remained suspended in air midway between the top and bottom of the bowl.

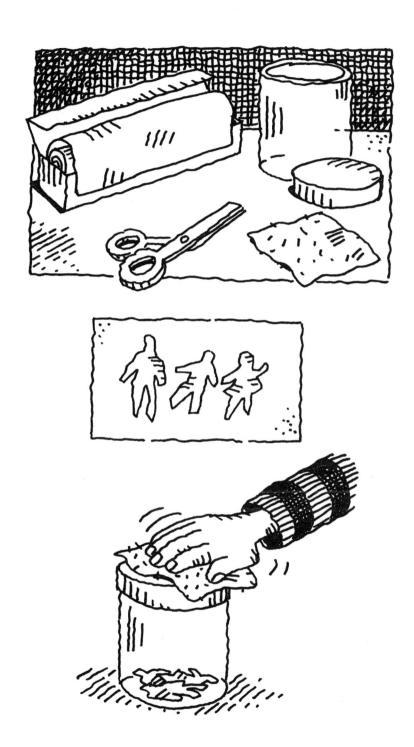

1.15 THE HUMIDITY CONNECTION

*S*ometimes, static electricity experiments work great. Other times, they seem to fizzle out. Here's an experiment that will help you explore how your surroundings affect static charge.

Materials
* *balloon*
* *bathroom*

To Do
Find a bathroom with a shower or bathtub. Make sure that no one has bathed in the room for several hours. The room's air should be dry.

Inflate a balloon. Charge the balloon by rubbing it on your hair. What charge does the balloon acquire? Place it against the wall. Observe how it clings to the surface.

Turn on the water in the shower or bathtub. Let the room fill with humid air. Now try charging the balloon again. Place it against the wall. What happens this time?

The Science
Electric charges cannot flow well through dry air. As the balloon was rubbed against the hair, charges moved onto the balloon. However, the dry air insulated the balloon and prevented the charges from "leaking" into the surrounding air.

Electric charges flow much better in humid air. When the air was humid, charges leaked from the balloon. Since the balloon lost its charge buildup, the clinging effect (if any) was not very great.

CHECK IT OUT! Do static electricity activities work better in winter or summer? Can you figure out why?

1.16 DOORKNOB ZAPS!

uch!

Materials
* *wool rug*
* *metal doorknob*

To Do
Find a room that has a rug and a metal doorknob. Turn off all of the lights and pull down the window shades. Put on your shoes and walk across the rug to the door.

Slowly bring your index finger towards the doorknob. What did you hear? What did you feel? What did you see?

The Science
As your shoes rub against the rug, negative charges leave it and enter your body. Although you don't feel it, your body takes on a net negative charge.

In nature, things like to be stable. Electric charges will move to create a stable, balanced condition.

As your hand nears the doorknob, negative charges concentrate at your fingertips. Just before you touch the knob, the charges have enough energy to "jump" across the gap. This jump produces a tiny spark. The spark heats up the air and produces a "snap."

CHECK IT OUT! Before an aircraft is fueled, a "grounding" wire must be contacted to the plane's body. Why?

1.17 CLOTHING ZAPS

*H*ave you ever tried to separate clothes that were just taken out of a drier? If so, you most likely encountered static cling. As the clothes were tossed in the drier, the materials rubbed against each other and transferred charges. Clothes that became oppositely charged stuck together.

Materials
* silk shirt
* wool sweater
* mirror

To Do
Put on a silk shirt. Pull a wool sweater over the shirt.

Find a room that has a mirror. Turn off all of the lights and pull down the window shades. The darker the room, the better the effect.

Stand a few feet in front of the mirror. Slowly roll up you sweater. What do you observe?

The Science
As the wool sweater rubbed against the silk shirt, charges were transferred. The shirt became negative in charge. The sweater lost electrons and became positive. The negative shirt and positive sweater attracted each other.

As you lifted the sweater, the charged materials separated. As they were pulled apart, visible sparks jumped the tiny gaps. These sparks produced a crackling sound.

ON YOUR OWN Find out what other material combinations produce sparks. Do some combinations work better than silk and wool?

1.18 DESIGNER RIP-OFFS

Sometimes tape is a pain to work with, especially if the weather is dry and the strips are long and lightweight. They seem to have a natural ability to attract each other. And once they make contact, their adhesive surface makes the problem even stickier. But is this attraction real or imagined? Why not find out!

Materials
* two 10-inch-long strips of tape
* cotton flannel shirt
* flat kitchen counter

To Do
Cut off two strips of tape. Each strip should be about 10 inches long. Press the strips against a flat flannel shirt. Keep one end of the strip free. After a moment, steadily pull both strips from the surface. Bring them near each other. What happens? Can you explain why?

Repeat the activity but this time press the strips against a kitchen counter top. Does the behavior of the strips change?

The Science
As the tape pulled away from its surface contact, charges were pulled up from the surface. Since both strips of tape acquired the same net charge, they repelled each other.

CHECK IT OUT! How could you use a strip of charged nylon to determine if the tape takes on a positive or negative charge?

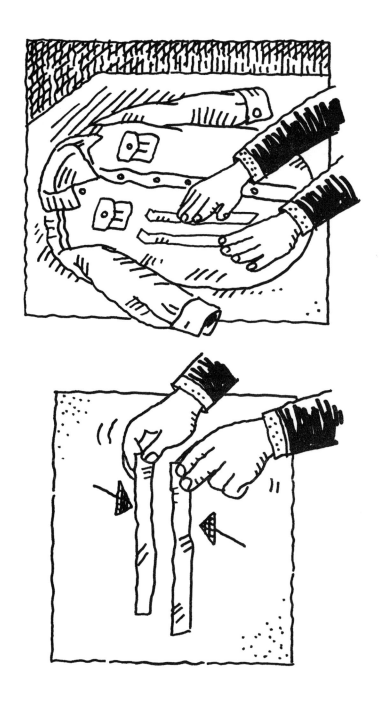

1.19 RADIO ZAPS

...O...S. As the *Titanic* sank, its radio officer sent out this distress call. Each click of the Morse code's key temporarily closed an electric circuit. This circuit produced a spark, which created an invisible energy wave that traveled out from the sinking ship. These waves were detected by the antennae of other boats. The antennae's signal was carried by wire to a receiver. There, the invisible waves were changed into an audible click.

Here's an experiment that illustrates how sparks were used to send Morse code messages. All you'll need is a carpet, doorknob, and wireless receiver (known nowadays as a radio).

Materials
* carpet
* metal doorknob
* radio

To Do
Switch on a radio. Tune the radio to a frequency where no signal is detected. With the volume turned up, the radio should broadcast a low level of static.

Walk across a wool carpet wearing a pair of shoes. Approach a doorknob. While listening to the radio, reach out and touch the knob. What do you hear on the radio?

The Science
Sparks create a form of energy called an electromagnetic wave. This wave travels outward through space. The antenna of a radio can detect this form of energy. The signals it captures are carried along wires to the radio's circuitry. There, the signals are turned into sound, which becomes amplified and broadcast through the radio's speakers.

CHECK IT OUT! Design an experiment that shows if sparks are detected by television sets.

1.20 STATIC SEPARATOR

The burning of fossil fuel produces air pollution. To prevent the release of soot, some stacks have anti-pollution devices called *electrostatic precipitators*. These devices place a static charge on the rising soot. As the soot continues to rise, it passes through oppositely-charged plates. The plates attract the soot and remove it from the smokestack gases.

Materials
* *plastic comb*
* *sugar*
* *pepper*
* *small plate*

To Do
Place two pinches of sugar and pepper side-by-side. Charge a comb by running it through your hair or stroking it with wool. Hold the comb several inches above the sugar and pepper. Slowly bring the comb closer to the mixture. Stop the comb when particles begin to jump onto it. Does sugar or pepper jump onto the comb first? Bring the comb closer to the mixture. Which particles jump onto the comb now?

The Science
Both pepper and sugar are attracted to the negatively-charged comb. However, because the pepper particles are lighter, they jump first onto the comb. As the comb is brought closer to the mixture, the force of attraction increases. Eventually, this force overcomes the greater weight of the sugar grains. Like the pepper, the sugar now jumps onto the comb.

CHECK IT OUT! Can a mixture of sugar and salt be separated by static charges?

1.21 STATIC JUMPERS

*P*uffed cereal grains are great materials for science experiments. Since they are light in weight, they do not require much force to move. In addition, the puffs easily transfer electric charges. Want to see? Just try this next experiment.

Materials
* *puffed cereal grains*
* *balloon*
* *a piece of wool or fur*

To Do
Stuff about a dozen grains of puffed cereal into a balloon. Inflate the balloon.

Rub the balloon with a piece of wool or fur. If the material isn't available, you can rub the balloon against your hair.

Hold the hanging balloon by its knot. Observe the grains within the balloon. Are they stationary or moving? Touch the balloon with the fingertips of your other hand. How do the grains behave? If nothing happens, recharge the balloon by giving it twice as many strokes. Then, touch it again.

The Science
As the balloon rubbed against the wool, it became negatively charged. Its negative field induced a positive charge in the nearby side of the puffed grains. This positive region was attracted to the balloon, causing the grains to cling to the balloon's negative skin.

When you touched the balloon with your fingertips, things changed. The balloon's negative charges drained out through your fingers. This created a positive region in the balloon. The charges in the grains could not shift fast enough. Instead, the positive grain surface and the positive balloon skin repelled each other. The grains jumped to another location.

CHECK IT OUT! Suppose a wooden rod touched the charged balloon. How would this affect the behavior of the puffed grains?

1.22 STATIC SHOWER

*U*p and down and up and down and up and...

Materials
* *section of Lucite*
* *two thick books (or stacks of smaller ones)*
* *puffed cereal or pieces of plastic foam*

HINT
If your hardware or lumber store doesn't carry Lucite, check out your stationery store. Many clipboards are made of Lucite instead of wood.

To Do
Place two thick books about 8 inches apart on a tabletop. The top of the books should reach several inches above the table.

Scatter puffed cereal grains or pieces of plastic foam in the gap between the books. Place a piece of Lucite across the gap so that it rests firmly on the books.

Rub a piece of wool or felt across the surface of the Lucite. What happens to the grains below? If you observed some movement, try rubbing your hand back-and-forth across the Lucite. To prevent the plastic section from slipping, you'll need to steady the Lucite with your other hand. Do the grains still move?

The Science
As you stroked the plastic, it became charged through contact. This plastic's negative field affected the charge balance in the cereal grains. The grains' nearby negative charges migrated towards the farther side of the grain. This created a positive end of each grain that was attracted to the plastic. This attraction caused the grains to jump upwards and cling to the Lucite.

While the grains were attached to the Lucite, the balance changed. Electrons in the plastic moved onto the grains. Although it took them several movements to transfer, this flow eventually canceled the grains' positive surface. Without this opposite charge, the grains were no longer attracted to the plastic. They dropped off because of their weight.

CHECK IT OUT! In the 1800s, a parlor game used this principle to toss dice. Can you build this game without seeing it?

HINT

Construct the dice from plastic foam.

1.23 GRAVITY-DEFYING PEANUTS

As the magician chanted the magic words, the rope responded. Slowly, it appeared above the basket's rim. Up went the rope. Higher and higher it climbed, until its entire length stretched before the audience.

Materials
* plastic foam "peanuts"
* 1-foot-long thread
* tape
* a piece of wool or fur
* balloon

To Do
Break off a segment of thread about a foot in length. Tie one end of the thread to the peanut. Tape the other end of the thread to the edge of a table. The peanut should hang down from the edge.

Rub the balloon with a piece of wool, fur, or your head. When the balloon is charged, slowly bring it closer to the peanut.

The peanut will be attracted to the balloon. As it moves closer to the balloon, slowly raise the balloon. Make sure that the peanut and balloon don't touch, or else an unwanted transfer of charges may occur. Keep raising the balloon until the peanut and thread extend perfectly upright. Keep raising the balloon. How far can it be raised and still support the peanut?

The Science
The peanut starts out with its charge distributed evenly over its length. The negatively charged balloon induces a positive peanut region. This positive region and the negative balloon attract.

Since the peanut and thread are relatively light, the force of attraction can produce an interesting effect: The peanut and thread overcome gravity and lift off the table.

CHECK IT OUT! Why would the thickness of the thread affect the height to which the peanut can be raised?

1.24 GET THE POINT?

A versorium is a device that is used to detect a static charge. Its name means "thing used for turning." It was given this name by its inventor about 400 years ago. Although times have changed, the principles that affected this tool haven't.

Materials
* *metal paper clip*
* *paper*
* *plastic comb or pen*
* *a piece of wool or felt*
* *a pair of scissors*

HINT
Doing the experiment in a transparent cup will prevent breezes from upsetting the versorium's delicate balance.

To Do
Unbend the larger arch of a paper clip. Position the smaller arch as a flat base. The unbent section should project straight up.

Draw the pattern shown below on a sheet of paper and use a pair of scissors to cut it out.

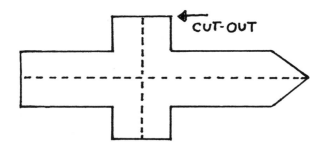

Put a slight downward crease along the dotted lines. Where they meet is the center of balance. Gently balance this pointer onto the paper clip.

Charge up a plastic comb or pen with a piece of wool or felt. Bring the pen close to the versorium. What do you observe? Can you get the pointer to spin in an entire circle?

The Science

The charged comb induced a positive region in the folded paper. This positive region and the negative comb attracted each other. The force was great enough to spin the pointer in any direction.

CHECK IT OUT! Can the needle of a versorium be made of aluminum foil?

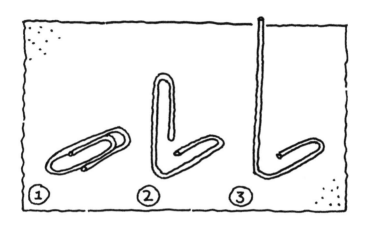

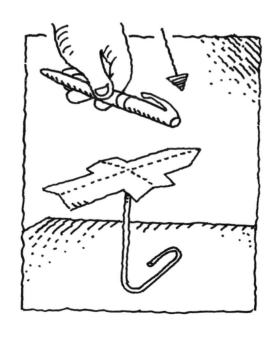

1.25 ON THE EDGE

*A*lthough gravity can be an incredible force, it requires huge masses to readily observe its effects. Not so with electricity. In fact, a minor charge can easily be observed using a tool that is often associated with uncovering an object's length.

Materials
* *wooden ruler*
* *balloon*

To Do
Position the wooden ruler so that it balances on the edge of a table. At this balance point, the ruler remains steady with one end slightly lifted from the tabletop.

Charge up the balloon by stroking it through your hair or with a piece of wool. Slowly approach the raised end of the ruler with the charged balloon. What happens? How does the electrostatic force work against the force of gravity?

The Science
When the ruler was balanced, it remained still. As the charged balloon was brought over one end of the ruler, it upset the wood's balance of charges. The negatively-charged balloon induced a positive charge in the near end of the ruler. This positive charge and the negative balloon attracted each other. The force of attraction was large enough to offset the balance of mass and cause the end of the ruler to rise up.

1.26 REPELLING PEANUTS

*A*s you've learned, like charges repel while unlike charges attract. You've also observed how charges can be transferred from one object to another. The following experiment uses both of these concepts. After building it, figure out how this tool might be used to measure charges.

Materials
* metal clothes hanger
* 12-inch-long thread
* two plastic foam "peanuts"
* balloon

To Do
Hold the hanger's hook with one hand. Firmly grasp the long side of the hanger with the other. Slowly and steadily stretch out the shape of the hanger until it looks like a stretched-out diamond.

Bend up one half of the diamond. The fold you produce will form a stand. Give the hook a quarter turn so that it falls back towards the center of the stand.

Tie a foam peanut to both ends of a 12-inch thread. Drape the thread across the upturned hook of the hanger. Position the thread so that the peanut hangs at the same level.

Inflate a balloon. Charge the balloon by rubbing it with a piece of wool or fur. Bring the balloon to the peanuts. How do the peanuts react? Touch the charged balloon to the peanuts. What happens now?

The Science
The lightweight peanuts were easily influenced by electric charges. When the balloon was brought nearby, it caused the charges within the peanuts to separate. The region of the peanuts nearest the balloon became positive and was attracted to the negative balloon.

When the peanuts were touched by the charged balloons, electrons flowed. These electrons caused both peanuts to become negatively charged. Since they had the same charges, the peanuts repelled each other. The repulsion produced enough force for the peanuts to separate and rise. The distance that they separated depended on how much charge they acquired. This distance can be used as a method for measuring charges.

CHECK IT OUT! Suppose the peanuts were placed on separate hanger supports. Would this affect their behavior?

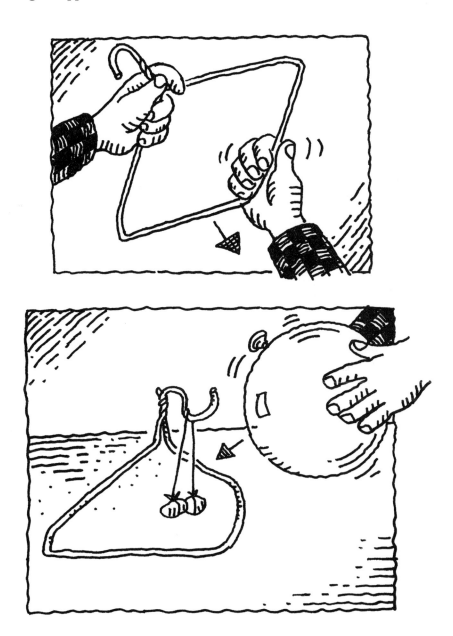

1.27 LIGHT THE LIGHT

Did you know that fluorescent lightbulbs are called "cool lights?" They get this name from the cool temperature at which they operate. Unlike regular filament bulbs, fluorescent lights don't need to heat up in order to produce light. The light that is given off by a fluorescent bulb comes from a special chemical that coats the glass. When this chemical is struck by charges, it lights up. Cool!

Materials
* *fluorescent lightbulb*
* *incandescent (filament) lightbulb*
* *piece of wool*
* *baloon*

To Do
Go into a dark room. Gently stroke the filament bulb with the wool. Observe its outer coating. Can you detect any light?

Now stroke the fluorescent bulb. After several minutes, examine its outer coating. What do you see? How does stroking each bulb affect the production of light?

Rub a balloon on your hair. Hold this charged balloon near the fluorescent bulb. What happens when a spark jumps between the bulb and the balloon?

The Science
An incandescent bulb needs to get "white hot" in order to produce light. In contrast, a fluorescent bulb doesn't depend upon heat in order to generate light. When the bulb was stroked by the wool, its surface became charged. As some of the charges jumped about, they excited the light-producing chemicals in the bulb's coating. These "energized" chemicals produced the faint glow of the bulb's surface.

1.28 FLYING LEAVES

*I*n the laboratory, scientists measure static charge with an *electroscope*. It is a tool that shows the relative strength of a charge. Here's an inexpensive version of an electroscope that you can build at home.

Materials
* *clear plastic cup*
* *two strips of aluminum foil*
* *metal paper clips*
* *modeling clay*
* *balloon*
* *pair of scissors*

HINT
The stout tumbler-type plastic cups work best!

To Do
Have an adult drill a small hole in the center of the cup's bottom. The hole must be wider than the wire of a paper clip.

Cut two small strips of aluminum foil. The strips should measure about ¼ inch × 1½ inch. Use an unbent paper clip to punch a tiny hole near the top of each strip. Press and flatten the foil. These foil pieces are called "leaves."

Open a paper clip and bend it to form a long "j." Hang the leaves on the bottom part of the "j." Insert the shaft of the paper clip into the underside of the cup. Make sure that the leaves clear the rim of the cup. Use a small lump of clay to secure the clip.

Roll up a piece of aluminum foil into a small ball. Place the ball on the shaft of paper clip that projects out of the cup. Set the cup on a table.

Charge a balloon by rubbing it with a piece of wool or fur. Slowly bring the balloon towards the cup. What happens to the leaves of the electroscope? Pull the balloon away. How do the leaves react?

The Science
As you brought the balloon near the electroscope, it induced a charge. The balloon's negative charge repelled the electrons that were in the ball of aluminum foil. These electrons traveled down the clip into the leaves. Both leaves acquired a negative charge. Since like charges repel, the leaves flew apart.

CHECK IT OUT! Design and construct a similar electroscope that uses a material other than aluminum foil.

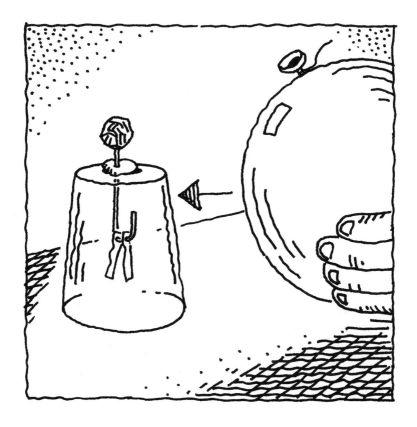

1.29 EGG-CENTRIC FINALE

Soap bubbles represent a delicate balance of forces. Water tension creates the force that holds the thin film of the bubble together. Soap within the bubble solution offsets these forces and allows the bubbles to stabilize. This results in a lightweight sphere whose shape is easily changed by static forces. Watch.

Materials
* bubble solution
* drinking straw
* mug or plastic container
* balloon

To Do
Fill a mug one-third full with bubble solution. Insert a straw into the solution. Blow into the solution with a slow and steady exhale. A mountain of bubbles should climb over the rim of the mug.

Charge a balloon by rubbing it through your hair. Move the balloon close to the bubbles. What happens? Describe how the bubbles becomes distorted. Is the attraction strong enough to "rip" a bubble from the mug?

The Science
Like the packaging "peanuts" and puffed cereal grains, soap bubbles react well to static charges. Their light weight and ease of charging make them an ideal subject for studying the effects of static attraction.

As the charged balloon approached the bubbles, the bubbles' nearby electrons reacted. These negatively charged particles migrated to the far side of the bubbles. This created a bubble top with a positive charge. The top was attracted to the negative balloon. This attraction caused the bubbles to stretch out and form an egg shape.

CHECK IT OUT! Will a bubble blown from a wand also react to a charged balloon? Make a guess and then find out.

PART TWO

CURRENT ELECTRICITY

WARNING! The activities in the following section should only be done with 1.5-volt flashlight cells. Do not use any other batteries, current sources, or electric outlets!

2.1 COMING TO TERMS

*D*o you get tired of reading instructions? Everyone does. Wouldn't it be great for the only instruction to be "HAVE FUN!" Well, this is it. There are no written instructional steps for this activity. All you have to do is mess around with the following parts. Who knows? You might light a bulb and, in the process, uncover a whole bunch of things about electricity.

Materials
* *one "D" cell battery*
* *connecting wires with each end stripped 1½ inches bare of insulation*
* *one flashlight bulb*

To Do
Have fun!*
If you're looking for a challenge, try lighting this bulb.

The Science
Since we are just having fun on this page, let's wait for the scientific explanation. Instead, let's clear up some confusion about names and terms.

Is it a battery or a cell?
    It depends upon who you are. Most people, who aren't scientists or science teachers, call these things batteries.
    "The flashlight needs more batteries."
    "The toy died. It needs a new set of batteries."
    People in science, however, tend to call these energy devices *cells*. The size (and electric force) of a cell is identified by letters. For example, the large cell that fits in a flashlight is a "D" cell. The smaller cells that power Walkmans™ are "AA" cells.
    Scientists use the term *battery* when there is more than one cell hooked together.

Is it a bulb or a lamp?
    Again, it depends upon how scientific you want to sound. Although most people call it a bulb, scientists call it a lamp. The lamp indicates

that this thing emits light. To scientists, a bulb can be anything from a flower part to a squishy rubber contraption.

What's meant by a cell's polarity?

All cells have a positive (+) pole and a negative (-) pole. In a household cell, the top (end with the central cap) is the positive pole, or positive terminal. The flat bottom end of the cell is the negative pole, or negative terminal. Electrons are pushed out of the cell at the negative pole and after traveling through the external circuit return to the cell at the positive pole.

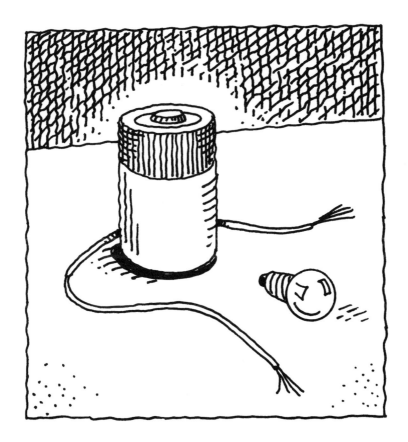

2.2 BATTERY HOLDER

*T*hink about the fun you had in the previous experiment. You probably wished that you had a few extra hands to hold down wires and keep things connected. Although we can't offer you a lab assistant (you'll have to build your own, Dr. Frankenstein), we can show you how to free up your hands by constructing some laboratory devices.

This first one is a battery (okay, or *cell*) holder.

Materials
* *thick rubber band that fits snugly over a battery*
* *two brass paper fasteners*
* *two 1-foot-long wires with each end stripped 1½ inches bare of insulation*

To Do
To make this battery holder, push a brass paper fastener into the middle of a thick rubber band. Bend back the "legs" so that the fastener remains anchored in the band as shown.

Insert a second fastener into the opposite end of the rubber band. Again, spread the legs back to secure the fasteners.

Flip the rubber band inside out so that the caps of the fasteners face inwards (the legs should be on the outer surface). Slip the rubber band over a cell. Attach one wire to each of the fasteners. Remember that the ends of the wire must be stripped of insulation in order to make electrical contact.

To test the holder, touch the free ends of the connecting wires to a flashlight bulb (okay, or *lamp*).

To make a double cell-holder, use a longer rubber band.

The Science

If the holder doesn't work, make sure that the legs of the clip and the connecting wire have an electric contact. The end of the wire should be free of any insulation. If you are using a bell wire (a thick wire that science teachers always seem to have), make sure to strip the plastic covering from the end of the wire. If you are using enamel-painted wire, you'll need to scrap off the painted surface with sandpaper or emery cloth. Then, make sure that the caps of the fasteners are positioned against the terminals of the cell.

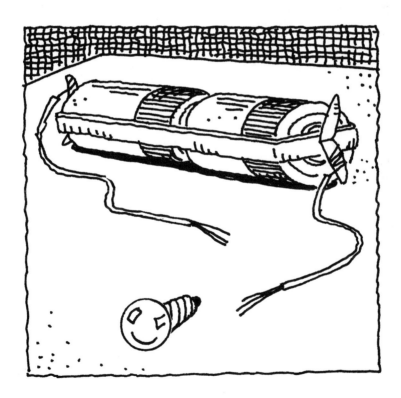

2.3 BULB HOLDER

*N*ow that your hands are free, let's build one more device: a bulb holder.

Materials
* *metal paper clip*
* *masking tape*
* *two connecting wires with each end stripped 1½ inches bare of insulation*
* *flashlight bulb*
* *"D" cell battery*

To Do
While holding a paper clip's outer loop, gently bend the inner loop downwards so it looks like this:

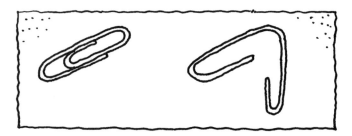

Form a wrapping of masking tape across the gap in the smaller loop. This wrapping should form a "ledge."

Wind the bare end of a wire around the wrapping. Make sure that the tape insulates the clip from the wire (see illustration).

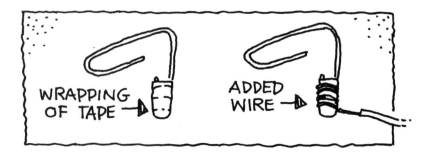

WRAPPING OF TAPE →

ADDED WIRE →

Wrap the bare end of a second wire around the bent region of the paper clip.

Insert a flashlight bulb into the larger loop. The threads of the bulb should fit snugly against the clip. As you turn the bulb, it should "screw" into the holder. The bottom terminal of the bulb should press firmly against the exposed wire wrap. You may have to bend the clip in order to adjust the contacts.

Once you have constructed the holder, test it by connecting the contact wires to a "D" cell. Don't worry if the light does not glow brightly. As long as it lights, your lamp holder is fine.

The Science

Let's discuss why your lamp didn't glow as brightly as you would have hoped. All lamps are designed for a specific voltage. Often this value is stamped on the bulb's metal collar. Most flashlight bulbs need 3 volts to shine their brightest. At lower voltages they emit less light. A single "D" cell has only 1.5 volts and, therefore, can't energize this lamp to its brightest state.

CHECK IT OUT! You can, however, buy bulbs that have been designed to shine brightest when connected to 1.5 volts.

NOTE
Never connect a bulb to more voltage than it is designed to handle. The extra voltage will produce a flow of current that can burn out the filament (thin thread inside the bulb) and destroy the bulb!

2.4 SWITCH

*T*ake a look around you. Most likely, there's a nearby wall switch (unless, of course, you're reading this book outdoors, or in a car, or train, or airplane, etc.).

Although you can't see it, the wall switch is connected to electrical wires that lead to a light fixture. When you flip the switch to the "on" position, the light goes on. Flip the switch "off" and the light magically goes off. Is this a simple coincidence or is there something more, something from beyond?

Materials
* a small block of wood
* two thumbtacks
* metal paper clip
* two connecting wires with each end stripped 1½ inches bare of insulation

To Do
Position two thumbtacks several inches apart on a small block of wood. Push them partially into the wood, leaving only a small space between the tacks' head and the wood surface.

Obtain two wires that have the insulation removed from both ends. Wrap a bare end from one of the wires around one of the thumbtacks. Push this tack into the wood to secure the wire.

Bend open a paper clip into an "S" shape. Slip one end of the paper clip's hook under the other thumbtack. Wrap this same thumbtack with the bare end of the second wire. Push this tack into the wood to secure both the wire and the paper clip.

Make sure that the paper clip extends over the other thumbtack. If not, bend it out some more. When you press down on the clip, it should make contact with the head of the first thumbtack. When you release, the clip should spring back up and "open" the circuit.

The Science
The flow of electricity requires an uninterrupted path through which electric charges will move. The charges will stop flowing if there are

any breaks in the path. It doesn't matter where the break is. As long as the path is not complete, no current will flow.

A switch is a device that can *open* and *close* a circuit. In the "on" position, the switch closes the circuit and completes the route for flowing current. In the "off" position, the switch places a gap in the path, which prevents any of the current from flowing.

2.5 DRAWING A CIRCUIT

*H*ow well do you draw? Do your lightbulbs look like lightbulbs or do they resemble the heads of aliens from outer space?

Although this next experiment involves drawing, don't worry. You don't have to be an artist. All you have to do is copy simple symbols and arrange them to represent electric circuits. So pick up your pencil and give it a try!

Materials
* *pencil*
* *a sheet of paper*

To Do
Examine the symbols below. They represent different parts of a circuit. Can you figure out what the complete circuit looks like? Look at the next page to find out.

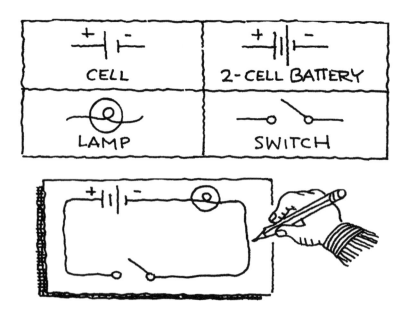

Now it's your turn. Use these symbols to draw diagrams that represent the following circuits. Don't forget about the polarity of each cell and how to illustrate it correctly.

The Science

Symbols are awesome. By the way, the answer is found at the bottom of page 81.

2.6 CONDUCTIVITY TESTER

lice a bell wire in half and you'll uncover a copper core surrounded by a plastic covering. It's the inner copper strand that offers the path for electron flow. The outer covering is a very poor conductor of electricity. It cloaks the copper to prevent electricity from traveling out of the wire and into other conductors (such as you—*ZAP!*).

Materials
* *"D" cell in battery holder*
* *flashlight bulb in lamp holder*
* *connecting wires with each end stripped 1½ inches bare of insulation*
* *a variety of materials, such as different coins, aluminum foil, compact disks, keys, costume jewelry, rings, and spoons*

To Do
Assemble the circuit shown on the next page. It's a conductivity tester that can show you if a material is a good or poor conductor of electricity.

Touch the bare ends of the two wires together and the lamp should light. If not, check your connections. Place the material to be tested on the tabletop. Touch the wires to opposite sides of the material. Make sure that the wires don't touch. Does the lamp light? If so, what do you know about the material's ability to offer a path for electron travel? Suppose the lamp doesn't light. What then?

The Science
Some materials, such as metals, are formed by atoms that have a *loose* hold on their electrons. Since the electrons are not tightly bound to individual atoms, they can be easily passed among neighboring atoms. The "passing" of electrons forms a movement of charge known as an electric current. Materials that permit easy electron flow are called *conductors*.

Other materials, such as glass and plastic, are formed by atoms that have a tight hold on their electrons. These atoms resist passing electrons from neighbor to neighbor. This resistance produces a material that acts as an *insulator*.

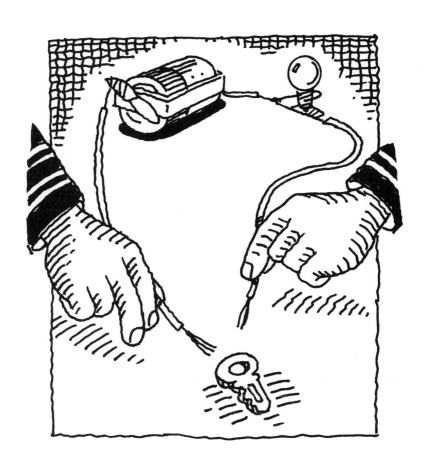

2.7 GET THE LEAD OUT

Dimmers are cool devices. Some of these circuit components are attached to ceiling lights or floor lamps. As you rotate the dimmer knob, the light gets brighter or dimmer.

Materials
* *pencil (or just a piece of pencil lead AKA graphite)*
* *two "D" cells in battery holders*
* *one flashlight bulb in lamp holder*
* *connecting wires with each end stripped 1½ inches bare of insulation*

To Do
Have an adult use a wood-carving tool to shave down one side of a pencil so that a long length of graphite is exposed. It should look like this:

If you can't find an adult to do the carving, do *not* do it yourself! Instead, you can use a piece of graphite that's meant for use in refillable pencils.

Assemble the circuit below.

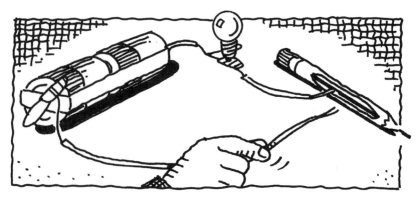

Touch the bare ends of the two wires together and the lamp should light. If not, check your connections. Now place the ends of both tester wires against the graphite. What happens? Slowly move these wires farther apart along the length of graphite. What happens to the brightness of the lamp? Can you explain your observations? Predict what will happen if the wires are moved together. Find out if your prediction is correct.

The Science

Unlike copper, graphite isn't a good conductor of electricity. When electricity flows through graphite, it crashes "head-on" into resistance. This resistance cuts down on the flow of electricity.

When your circuit included only a small section of graphite, the lamp remained bright. As the wires were drawn apart, the current was forced to travel a greater distance through the graphite path. This extra distance produced increased resistance, which cut down the electricity and made the bulb dimmer.

ANSWER TO EXPERIMENT 2.5

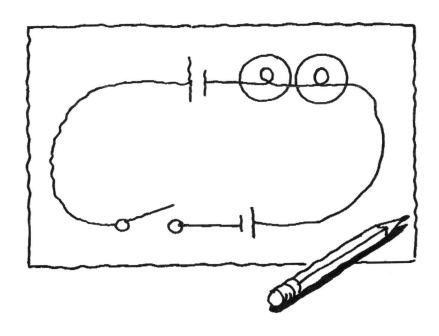

2.8 SHORT CIRCUIT

OP QUIZ

Question: What would happen if you were to connect the positive and negative terminals of a cell together without placing a bulb, motor, or some sort of resistance in the circuit?

Answer: If the circuit were left on for more than a few minutes, you'd ruin the cell (and if the current source was large enough, you'd burn yourself or start a fire).

Materials

* two "D" cells in battery holders
* one flashlight bulb in lamp holder
* two switches
* connecting wires with each end stripped 1½ inches bare of insulation

To Do

Assemble the circuit below.

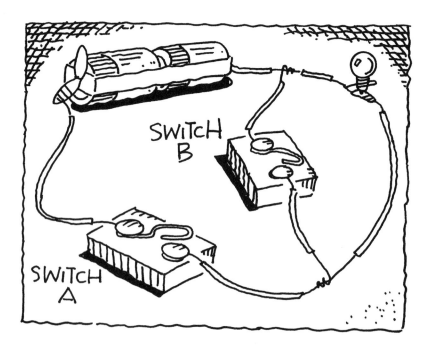

Close only switch A. What happens to the lamp? Is there a closed circuit? If so, trace the complete circuit through which electricity flows.

Close only switch B. What happens to the lamp? Is there a closed circuit? If so, trace the complete circuit through which electricity flows.

Bend the clip in switch A so that this switch remains on. While the lamp is glowing, close switch B. What happens? What path does the current follow when both switches are closed? Why? Release switch B. What happens now? Why?

The Science

Switch A controls current flow in the outer loop. When switch A is closed, current flows along this outer path to light the lamp.

Switch B is part of a separate path that offers no resistance. When switch B was closed, its path became complete. Since the path contained no resistors, it acted as a short circuit. The current flowed across switch B and bypassed the lamp. Without a current flow, the lamp went out.

CHECK IT OUT! Short circuits can cause fires. When a wire offers little or no resistance to current flow, excessive current flow can heat up the conductor. If the wire gets hot enough, it can cause burns and fires.

2.9 A LIMITED PATH

*H*ave you ever tested old batteries in a 2-cell flashlight? If so, you know that both of the cells need to be working. If one cell has leaked, the flashlight won't work. No matter how strong the other cell is, if one cell is bad the light won't go on. That's because the electricity needed to light the bulb must flow through both cells. If one cell is dead, the path is blocked. There's no way around it.

Materials
* two "D" cells in battery holders
* two flashlight bulbs in lamp holders
* switch
* connecting wires with each end stripped 1½ inches bare of insulation

To Do
Assemble the setup shown below.

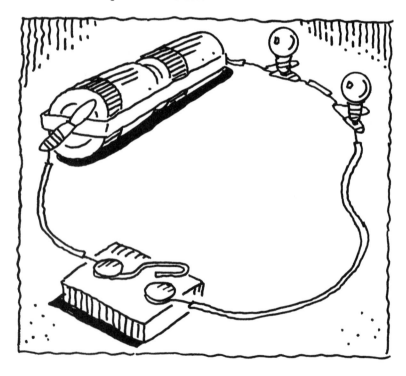

Close the switch. What happens? Do both bulbs light? Is one bulb brighter than the other? In this circuit, how many different paths can the electrons flow through?

Keep the switch closed. Unscrew one of the bulbs. What happens? Can you explain your observations?

Draw a diagram of this circuit using the symbols presented earlier. Use this diagram to describe the flow of electrons.

The Science

The circuit you built is called a *series circuit*. It offers only one path for the moving charges. All the electrons must travel through the same circuit components.

If one of the wires is broken (or one of the components removed), the circuit is opened. All current stops! That's why the other bulb went out, even though it remained attached to the circuit.

2.10 A PATH WITH MORE OPTIONS

*H*ave you ever been to a party that was lit up by strings of overhead lights? You know the type. Sets of these lights hang as holiday or patio decorations. Years ago, all of the bulbs, except for their colors, looked similar. Now you can buy bulbs that resemble everything from peppers to parrots.

As you may have observed, some of these light sets are hooked up in a special way. When one bulb goes out, the others remain lit! This way of wiring makes it much easier to identify the burned-out bulb. Otherwise, you'd be faced with testing the entire set.

Materials
* *two "D" cells in battery holders*
* *two flashlight bulbs in lamp holders*
* *connecting wires with each end stripped 1½ inches bare of insulation*
* *switch*

To Do
Assemble the setup shown below.

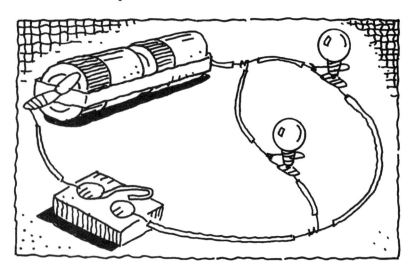

Close the switch. What happens? Do both bulbs light? Is one bulb brighter than the other? In this circuit, how many different paths can the electrons flow through?

Keep the switch closed. Unscrew one of the bulbs. What happens? Can you explain your observations?

Draw a diagram of this circuit using the symbols presented earlier. Use this diagram to describe the flow of electrons.

The Science

The circuit you built is called a *parallel circuit*. It offers more than one path for the moving charges. This circuit had two possible paths. The current of flowing electrons split up. Half the current traveled through the nearer "arm" of the circuit. The other half traveled through the distant "arm."

This time, when a bulb was removed, the remaining bulb stayed lit. That's because the path to the untouched bulb remained intact. The electrons continued to flow along this smaller but complete circuit loop.

2.11 THE BASIC BUZZER

I t's time for a break. Instead of resting, however, you get to assemble a simple circuit. This working circuit will be used in several of the following experiments. Right now, you need to find the components, make sure they match up, and assemble the circuit correctly.

Materials
* buzzer or bicycle horn (1.5-volt or 3-volt device)
* one or two "D" cell batteries
* battery holders
* connecting wires with each end stripped 1½ inches bare of insulation
* wire stripper

CAUTION
Do not use any buzzer that requires more than two "D" cell batteries.

To Do
Find a buzzer or bicycle horn. Buzzers can sometimes be removed from old board games that have "buzzing" sounds. If you do remove the buzzer from a game, write down the type and number of cells needed to energize the buzzer. Remember, you'll need to match your battery supply to the electrical needs of this device.

If you don't find a board game buzzer, a bicycle horn might work. Some horns can be removed from their streamlined case. If so, you'll need to identify the terminals to the horn. If the horn can't be separated from the case, remove the cell. Attach wires to the terminals that are exposed inside the battery holder. These wires can then be attached to your circuit as direct paths to the buzzer. Again, you'll need to match up the horn with the correct power supply.

And if all else fails, there's always the local electronics store. They should have both 1.5-volt and 3-volt buzzers.

Your simple circuit should look like what's shown on the following page. In the following experiments, you'll need to add this circuit to different types of switches. Before you do, make sure that the buzzer works.

The Science

When the circuit is complete, electricity flows. This current of electrical charges "energizes" the horn, which causes its sound-producing parts to vibrate. We detect the vibrations as a BUZZZZZ.

2.12 SECRET SWITCH

Alarm systems are cool, especially the high-tech ones that detect an intruder by the heat he or she gives off. In this experiment, you'll get to construct an alarm device and use it to assemble a circuit.

Materials
* *two connecting wires with each end stripped 1½ inches bare of insulation*
* *simple buzzer circuit (see p. 88)*
* *10 inch × 3 inch cardboard*
* *pair of scissors*
* *2-inch strip of aluminum foil*
* *tape*

To Do
Cut out a strip of cardboard (removed from a packing box) that is about 10 inches long × 3 inches wide. Bend the strip in half to form two 5-inch-long sections. Wrap the middle of each section with a 2-inch strip of aluminum foil. Use tape to secure the strip. Attach two 1-foot-long wires to the outer side of each strip. These wires are attached to a series circuit that contains two 1.5-volt cells and a buzzer. The folded cardboard should be placed beneath a carpet or mat. Make sure that the weight of the carpet doesn't close the halves together. Once the alarm detector is "set," just sit back and wait.

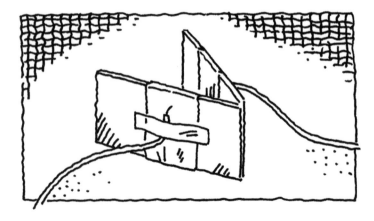

The Science

The alarm detector is a pressure switch. The weight of the carpet is not great enough to fully press the cardboard halves together. Therefore, the switch remains open. When someone stands on the carpet, however, their added weight closes the switch. Once closed, the current can flow from the battery to the buzzer and sound the alarm!

2.13 DOOR ALARM

*H*ave you ever seen a cartoon in which someone removes a tooth by using a string tied to a doorknob? As the door slams shut, the string tugs at the attached tooth. This "pull" is great enough to yank the tooth out of its socket. Ouch!

Materials

* connecting wires with each end stripped 1½ inches bare of insulation
* simple buzzer circuit (see p. 88)
* 5 inch × 3 inch cardboard
* pair of scissors
* metal paper clip
* tape
* two metal thumbtacks
* string
* small square piece of paper

To Do

Cut out a strip of cardboard (removed from a packing box) that is about 5 inches long × 3 inches wide. Push two metal thumbtacks into the cardboard. The tacks should be about 2 inches apart. Wrap a length of conducting wire around the shaft of each tack.

Unbend a paper clip into an "S" shape. Slip one end of the clip around the base of one tack. Adjust the bend in the clip to ensure that there is enough pressure to keep the far end of the clip pressed down on the other tack.

Slip a small square of paper between the clip and the tack. The paper will be held in place by the pressure of the bent clip.

Tape a string to the paper. Tie the other end of the string to a doorknob. Attach the conducting wires to a series circuit that contains two 1.5-volt cells and a 3-volt buzzer.

Tape the cardboard setup down so that it remains secure. Now invite a friend to open the door. BUZZZZZZZZZZZZ.

The Science

The paper that was inserted between the clip and the tack acted as an insulator. This insulator blocked the flow of electric current. When the paper was yanked away, the clip and tack made contact. When the circuit became complete, charges flowed and the alarm sounded.

2.14 STEADY HANDS

*H*ave you ever played the electrified board game in which you must operate on a patient? If your hand isn't steady, the forceps strike the conducting metal. Instantly a loud sound confirms that you "grounded out" and completed your turn. In this experiment, you'll have the chance to build another type of game that also tests your steadiness.

Materials
* metal clothes hanger
* simple buzzer circuit (see p. 88)
* two lumps of clay
* connecting wires with each end stripped 1½ inches bare of insulation
* steel wool

To Do
Use steel wool to remove any sort of coating or lacquer that covers the clothes hanger. Make sure that you remove this coating outdoors and don't breath in any of this material.

Untwist the coat hanger and rebend it into a large "U." Make several bumps in the middle section of the "U." Stand up the ends of this clothes hanger with lumps of clay.

Assemble the battery of two "D" cells. Attach a connecting wire from one base of the clothes hanger to one terminal of the buzzer. Attach another connecting wire from the other terminal of the buzzer to one of the ends of the battery. Now attach the 2-foot-long connecting wire to the other end of the battery. Bend the free end of the 2-foot wire into a small loop that fits around the coat hanger.

The object of this game is to move the loop along the entire path and not make contact with the hanger.

The Science
In order to "win," you have to maintain an open circuit. If your hand is not steady, the loop will make contact with the conductive hanger. Once contact is made, the circuit becomes complete and the buzzer sounds to announce your defeat!

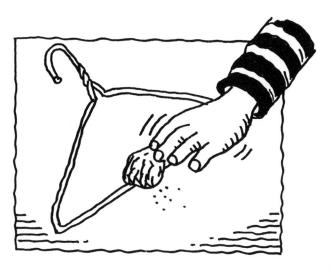

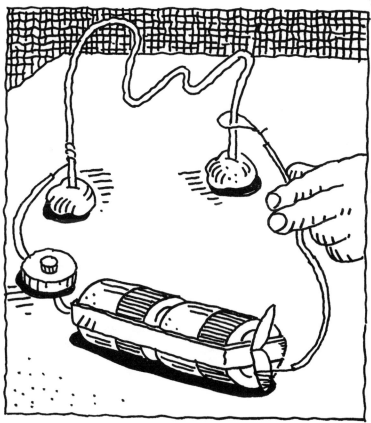

2.15 THE MAGNETIC CONNECTION

*E*lectricity-carrying cables are often buried underground. To locate their exact position, utility workers use a tool that detects magnetic fields. Within the cables, a current of flowing charges produces a magnetic field that extends into the surrounding space. By uncovering this magnetic field, workers can locate the exact position of the unseen electric flow.

Materials

* *two "D" cells in battery holders*
* *connecting wires with each end stripped 1½ inches bare of insulation*
* *switch*
* *index card*
* *iron filings*
* *compass*

To Do

Assemble the complete circuit shown below. Place an index card on top of a section of wire so that you just can't see it.

Turn the switch to the "on" position for a few minutes only. Otherwise, you will damage the cell. Lightly sprinkle iron filings onto the card. Tap the card gently. Do the filings form a pattern or do they scatter randomly? Can you explain your observations?

Turn the switch to the "off" position. Carefully return the iron filings to their container.

Place a compass alongside the wire. Note the direction that the needle points. While watching the needle, turn the switch to the "on" position. What do you observe? Explain what you see.

Suppose you switched the connectors to the cells so that their polarity was reversed. How would that affect the direction in which the needle points? Make a guess and then find out by switching the connections. Was your guess correct?

The Science

Electric currents produce a detectable magnetic field. The filings that fell onto the index card "felt" the force of the magnetic field. Their final position formed a pattern that followed the magnetic lines of force that extended outward from the wire.

Likewise, the compass needle also "felt" the magnetic force. When the current flowed, it produced a magnetic attraction that successfully competed with the Earth's magnetic field.

2.16 UPSTAIRS/ DOWNSTAIRS SWITCH

Did you hear that? It sounds like a saliva-dripping alien monster sloshing around at the bottom of the stairs—or maybe it's just a dog."

"Should I turn on the light?"

"Sure. But I'm not going down there."

"No need to. There's a light switch right here at the top of the stairs."

Materials
* *two "D" cells in battery holders*
* *one flashlight bulb in lamp holder*
* *six thumbtacks*
* *two metal paper clips*
* *two pieces of wood or thick foam core*
* *connecting wires with each end stripped 1½ inches bare of insulation*

To Do
For this activity, you'll need to build two new switches. The switch bases are made from two small blocks of wood. Carefully push three thumbtacks partially into the wood base as shown below. Bend apart a paper clip and wrap it around the thumbtack that is on the side by itself. Don't push the tacks fully into the wood until the wire connections are in place.

Now assemble the circuit below using these two switches. Unlike the previous switches, these circuit parts are sliding switches. The clip is constantly pushed against the top of the tack or wood surface. When you slide the bent clip onto a tack, you complete a circuit. This circuit remains "on" until you slide the clip off the tack.

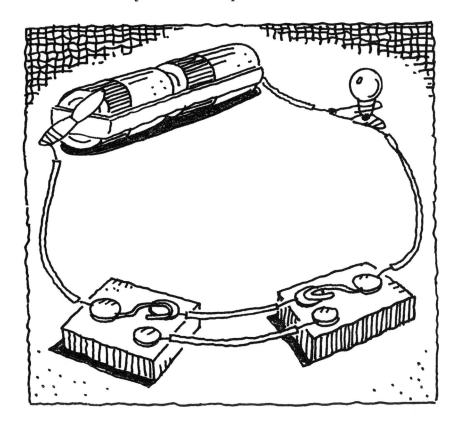

Flip one switch. What happens? Flip the other switch. What happens now? Which switch controls the lamp? Explain.

The Science

The circuit is constructed so that both switches form the path over which the electric current must flow. If either switch is flipped, the circuit will change. If it was open, a flipped switch will close the circuit. If it was closed, a flipped switch will open the circuit. As you might infer, this type of switch is useful when you want to control a light from two different locations.

2.17 MEET A METER

An electrician usually uses a special tool to measure the current that flows through a wiring. The tool is called a *multimeter* and it is capable of measuring several properties of electric flow. In this experiment, you'll get to build a simple type of meter that will also respond to the flow of current.

Materials
* *10 yards of 24-gauge insulated copper wire*
* *wire strippers*
* *packaging tape*
* *sewing needle*
* *thread*
* *strong bar magnet*
* *juice can*
* *"D" cell battery*

To Do
Strip several inches of insulation from both ends of the wire. Wrap this wire around the can into a tight coil, leaving about a foot of wire at each end of the coil. Slip the coil off the can. Wrap several pieces of packaging tape around the coil to secure its shape. Use a larger piece of tape to tape the coil onto a flat surface so that it stands up.

Use the magnet to magnetize the sewing needle. Stroke the needle at least forty times in the same direction.

Tie a small length of thread around the middle of the needle so that it balances. Tape the other end of the thread to the top of the wire coil. The magnetized needle should balance in the middle of the coil's open space.

Touch the free ends of the wires to the positve and negative sides of the "D" cell battery. What happens? Switch the wires and touch the opposite sides of the cell. What happens now?

The Science
When the wires were attached to the cell, electricity flowed through the coil. This movment of charge created a magnetic field. The mag-

netic field affected the magnetized needle, causing it to spin and change its pointing direction. When the wires were switched, the current flowed in the opposite direction. In response, the needle turned and pointed in the opposite direction.

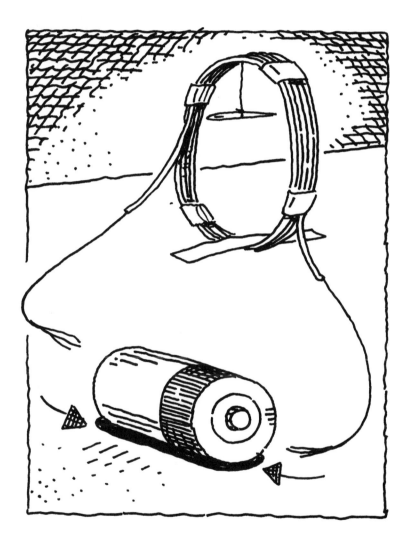

2.18 FRUIT CELL

*H*ave you ever heard of a potato clock? If so, you probably know that this device uses two potatoes to generate the energy for the clock's circuit. Right? Wrong. The potatoes don't generate the electrical flow. The potatoes are merely solid structures through which charges can flow. The parts that produce the flow of charges are the two different metals that are stuck into the potato. Want to learn more? Read on.

Materials
* *lemon*
* *copper penny*
* *strip of zinc (obtained from hardware store)*
* *steel wool*
* *knife*
* *current meter (assembled in "Meet a Meter" experiment, p. 100)*

To Do
Use the steel wool to shine the surfaces of the penny and the zinc strip. File down any sharp edges of the zinc strip.

Have an adult use the knife to punch two small slits into the lemon's tough skin. The slits should be about ½ inch in length and placed about ¼ inch apart.

Insert a penny into one of the slits. Insert the zinc strip into the other slit. Make sure that the metals don't touch.

Touch the leads of the current meter to the exposed metals. What happens to the magnetized needle? Can you explain your observation?

The Science
There is a natural tendency for electric charges to travel between two different metals (in this case copper and zinc). Within the lemon, the acid environment offered a partial route for the travel of charges. The route was completed by the external circuit, which included the coiled wire. As the current traveled through this coil, it produced a magnetic field. This field deflected the needle from its original pointing direction.

CHECK IT OUT! Can other pairs of metals also produce a detectable current? Try replacing the zinc with an "old" silver dime or a wad of aluminum foil.

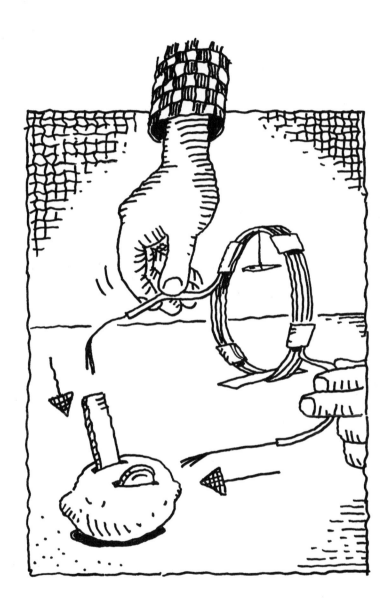

2.19 BATTERY OF CELLS

A single cell made of two metals can produce only a small "push" of charge. To increase this push, several cells can be wired together. This arrangment of side-by-side cells forms an electrical device known to scientists as a *battery*.

Materials
* *three pennies*
* *three iron washers*
* *steel wool*
* *blotter paper*
* *pair of scissors*
* *salt*
* *water*
* *current meter (assembled in "Meet a Meter" experiment, p. 100)*

To Do
Polish the surface of the coins and washers with steel wool. Use a pair of scissors to cut the blotter paper into four penny-sized circles.

Soak the paper in salt water. Sandwich a damp paper circle between a penny and a washer. Test the generation of electricity with your current meter. How does the meter react?

Make two other sandwiches. Stack all three sandwiches into a pile of alternating penny/wet paper/washer units. Insert a saltwater-soaked paper between the penny of one cell and the washer of its neighbor. In other words, no two coins should make direct contact.

Use tape to secure this three-cell stack. Retest the current. Is it stronger? Can you explain your observations?

The Science
The simple penny/washer cell produced a very small amount of electricity. As the cells were joined together, they formed a battery. The three-cell battery generated three times the electricity of a single cell. This increase produced a more noticeable deflection of the meter's needle.

CHECK IT OUT! A car battery is made of six side-by-side but separate cells. These cells are wired together to produce six times the energy available from only a single cell.

2.20 GENERATING A CONNECTION

So far, the electricity you've generated has been produced by chemical reactions. Although this source of electricity is important, most of your home is supplied by electricity that has been produced by generators. Generators are large devices that change the energy of spinning magnetic fields into electric current.

Materials
* *strong bar magnet*
* *10 yards of 24-gauge insulated copper wire*
* *juice can*
* *tape*
* *current meter (assembled in "Meet a Meter" experiment, p. 100)*

To Do
Strip several inches of insulation from both ends of the wire. Wrap this wire around the can into a tight coil. Leave about a foot of wire at each end of this coil. Slip the coil off the can and secure its shape with several pieces of tape. Attach the bare ends of these wires to the ends of the current meter's wires. A complete circuit containing two coils should be formed.

Push the bar magnet in and out of the newly assembled coil. What happens to the needle that is suspended in the current meter? Can you explain your observations?

The Science
Congratulations! You've just generated electricity. As the magnet moved in and out of the coil, it induced a back-and-forth flow of charges within the coil. This flow moved throughout the circuit. At the meter, this alternating current produced a flip-flopping magnetic field. Its effects were seen by the needle, which continually changed directions.

2.21 IT'S A WRAP!

se your bar magnet today. Put it away. If you take it out tomorrow, most likely it will still be a magnet. Take it out the next day and you'll find that it still has magnetic properties. That's why it's called a *permanent magnet*. But permanent doesn't mean forever. Over time, the magnet will lose its magnetic strength.

Materials
* *connecting wires with each end stripped 1½ inches bare of insulation*
* *pencil*
* *nail*
* *two "D" cells in battery holders*
* *switch*

To Do
Wrap a length of bell wire around a pencil so that it forms a tight coil. Make sure to leave plenty of wire free at each end so that the coil can be attached to a circuit.

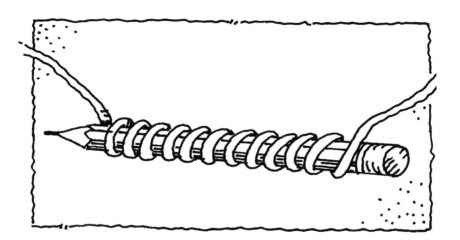

Once the coil is made, slip it off the pencil and use it to construct the circuit on the next page.

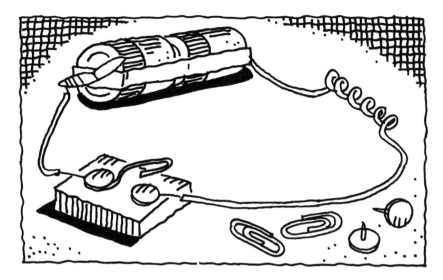

Close the switch. Touch the coil to some small paper clips or thumb-tacks. What happens? Can the coil lift these items? Release the switch. What happens now?

Slip an iron nail into the coil (see illustration). Tighten the coil around the nail by pulling on the wire ends. Now close the switch and try to pick up some clips or thumbtacks. What happens? How has the presence of an iron core affected the magnetic strength of this coil?

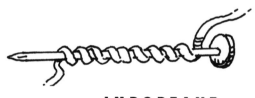

IMPORTANT
Turn this circuit on for *only* a few minutes at a time. Then turn it off. Otherwise, the cells will become ruined.

The Science
The flowing current creates a magnetic field. The field can by increased by wrapping the straight wire into a coil. It can be boosted even further by inserting an iron core into the center of the coil.

CHECK IT OUT! Some junkyards use giant electromagnets. At the flick of a switch, these awesome magnets can pick up or drop huge automobiles and vans.

2.22 MORSE CODE TRANSMITTERS

For our last electrical experiment, we will construct a Morse code station.

Materials
* four "D" cells in battery holders
* two flashlight bulbs in lamp holders
* two switches
* four brass fasteners
* plenty of connecting wire with ends stripped bare of insulation

To Do
Assemble two separate Morse code stations that look like this:

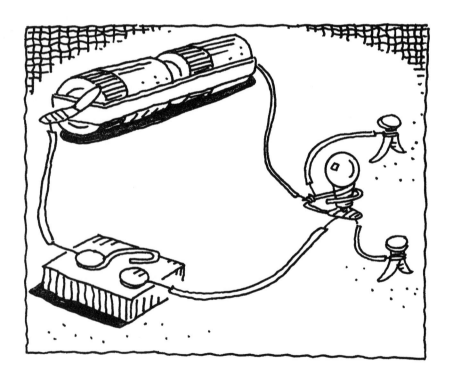

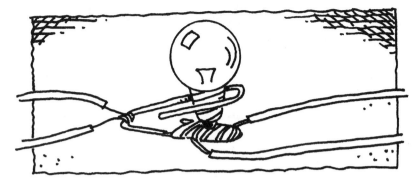

Next, place the two stations at different locations and connect them by wire. Begin by setting them up side-by-side. This will make solving any sort of connection problem much easier and quicker.

Use two lengths of connecting wire to attach the stations as shown here.

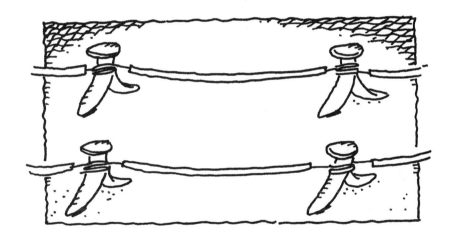

If this short connection works, you're ready to expand. Use more connecting wire and place the stations at opposite ends of your room. Do the transmitters still work? If so, you're ready.

Have an adult help you set up a pair of wires that will connect two stations that are placed in different rooms of the house.

IMPORTANT
Make sure that connecting wires aren't placed where they will get in the way and accidentally trip someone.

Make two photocopies of the Morse code sheet below. Keep a copy by each station.

A	B	C	D	E	F	G
•▬	▬•••	▬•▬•	▬••	•	••▬•	▬▬•

H	I	J	K	L	M	N
••••	••	•▬▬▬	▬•▬	•▬••	▬▬	▬•

O	P	Q	R	S	T	U
▬▬▬	•▬▬•	▬▬•▬	•▬•	•••	▬	••▬

V	W	X	Y	Z	ERROR
•••▬	•▬▬	▬••▬	▬•▬▬	▬▬••	••••••••

1	2	3	4	5
•▬▬▬▬	••▬▬▬	•••▬▬	••••▬	•••••

6	7	8	9	0
▬••••	▬▬•••	▬▬▬••	▬▬▬▬•	▬▬▬▬▬

Below each letter and number is the code that represents it. The circles are "dots." A dot is transmitted by a quick ON/OFF press of the switch. The small rectangles are "dashes." A dash is transmitted by a longer ON/OFF press.

This code was developed by a man named Samuel Morse. In 1838, Sam invented the first device that could send coded messages along electric wires. Soon everyone was calling these wire messages *Morse code.*

The Science

When either switch (called a *key* by Morse code people) is closed, the double-lamp circuit becomes complete. The current flows from the closest pair of cells through the large connecting loop of wire (that is strung between the stations). Flowing along this wire, the electricity lights both lamps. By monitoring your own bulb, you can make sure that your message has been sent to the other station. When you see a light, they will see a light.

MAGNETS AND MAGNETISM

3.1 FIELD TRIP

Close your eyes and think of a refrigerator door. What comes to mind? For most of us, we think of all sorts of paper—math tests, history reports, and grocery lists—hanging on the door by an assortment of magnets.

Although magnets and refrigerator doors seem inseparable, magnets can also attach themselves to many other objects and materials. To begin our first adventure into the field of magnetism, let's take a field trip. Although it might be nice to visit an exotic tropical island, all we need can be found in your kitchen.

Materials
* *refrigerator magnet*
* *paper*
* *pencil*

To Do
Remove a magnet from the refrigerator door. Pick one that is large and strong. You'll use this magnet to find out which of the following kitchen materials and objects are attracted to it. Make sure to test the following things and record your findings on a sheet of paper:
* refrigerator door handle
* other refrigerator magnets
* sink basin
* sink water faucet
* plastic wrap
* crumbled aluminum foil (without mustard or mayonnaise)
* spoon
* cooking pot
* frying pan
* copper water pipe
* food cans
* doorknob
* cabinet latches

The Science

As you've discovered, the magnet isn't attracted to all objects and materials. The ability for an object (metal or not) to be attracted by a magnet depends upon the material's composition. You'll learn more about what is and isn't attracted to magnets as you try a whole bunch of fun and interesting activities.

3.2 INVISIBLE SIGHTS

*H*ave you ever seen a science fiction show about an invisible monster or alien? If so, what trick did the hero use to finally "see" the monster? Was the monster splattered with paint? Was it coated with water? Perhaps its outline could be shown by the way its force field distorted the surrounding air.

Although magnetic fields may not be as dangerous as invisible aliens, they can be just as interesting. The only problem is that you can't see them—or can you?

Materials
* *paper*
* *iron filings*
* *bar magnet*

To Do
Position a bar magnet beneath a sheet of paper. Make sure that the paper remains level.

Lightly sprinkle iron filings over the paper. Tap the paper. Observe the pattern that they make as they fall onto the surface. Does the pattern contain straight or curved lines? Do these lines completely encircle the magnet? If not, where do the lines of force meet the magnet?

The Science
All magnets are surrounded by an invisible pattern formed by the magnet's lines of force. Although the lines, force, and the field are invisible, we can splatter it with a covering of magnetic materials.

Iron filings are light, small, and readily attracted to magnets. The filings that fell onto the paper formed a pattern that mirrored the lines of force that made up the magnetic field.

CHECK IT OUT! Guess what magnetic pattern a horseshoe magnet will produce. Then check it out with a magnet and filings.

3.3 MAPPING OUT MAGNETIC FIELDS

*H*ave you ever bought a foul-tasting cereal just to get the prize that was buried at the bottom of the box? Of course, you have. Everyone has! Yucch!

If you were lucky enough to uncover a compass, you're all prepared for this next activity—unless of course you've already lost, squished, or crushed it. But if it's still in one piece, the compass has more than a navigational use. It's a handy tool for mapping out invisible magnetic fields.

Materials
* *bar magnet*
* *compass*
* *paper*
* *pencil*

To Do
Place a magnet in the center of a sheet of paper and carefully trace out its shape. Bar magnets are rectangular.

Now place the compass on the same sheet of paper a few inches from the magnet. Draw its outline onto the paper. Observe the direction that the compass needle points. Pick up the compass and draw the direction in which the needle was pointing. Place the compass in another nearby spot. Again, trace its outline and draw in the direction of the needle. Keep going until a pattern emerges.

The Science
A compass needle is a tiny, lightweight magnet. It reacts to both Earth's magnetic field and to the fields of any nearby magnets. When it was placed close to the bar magnet, the needle rotated so that it aligned with the invisible field of the magnet. By moving the compass, you were able to uncover the extent and direction of the bar magnet's lines of force.

3.4 MAGNETIC METALS

From the first experiment, you've discovered that not all metals were attracted to magnets. Some, such as the refrigerator door handle, had strong magnetic properties. Others, such as wads of crumpled aluminum foil, lacked this attraction.

So what's the story with metal? Why are some metals attracted to magnets, while others have no reaction?

Materials

* *strong kitchen magnet*
* *an assortment of metal items such as a metal paper clip, steel nail, brass screw, stripped cooper wire, stainless steel utensil, penny, nickel, dime, quarter, and any other materials whose magnetic properties you aren't sure of*

To Do

Test the above objects to uncover whether they have magnetic properties. Steadily bring a magnet near the object. Does the object move? Is the attraction strong enough to lift the object? What force must be overcome if the magnet is to lift the object off the desktop?

The Science

All materials are made up of tiny building blocks called atoms. Every atom has its own magnetic field, which is produced by its moving electrons. In most materials, the tiny atomic fields point in completely random directions. Because of their randomness, these tiny fields cancel each other out (one pulls right, another pulls left, one pulls down, another pulls up, etc.).

The magnetic fields of a few materials, such as iron and nickel, can be made to all point in the same direction. So instead of canceling out each other's force, the forces add up and make the material magnetic.

CHECK IT OUT! The composition of U.S. coins has changed over the years. Have any coins ever been magnetic? In what years?

3.5 MAKING A MAGNET

*S*uppose the smallest of all particles acts like a tiny, free-spinning magnet. Now imagine a material composed of a vast landscape of these side-by-side force fields. If all of the individual magnetic fields pointed in different directions, they'd cancel each other out. Some would pull in one direction, others would pull in another. However, if all of the fields pointed in the same direction, the individual forces would add together and produce what we call *magnetism*.

Materials
* *iron nails*
* *bar magnet*
* *magnetic compass*

To Do
Hold a magnet several inches from a magnetic compass. Move the magnet and observe any movement of the compass needle. What happens to the needle as the magnet is moved?

Hold an iron nail several inches from the compass. Move the nail and observe any movement of the compass needle. What happens to the needle as the nail is moved?

Now hold the nail in one hand and the bar magnet in the other. Stroke the magnet along the length of the nail. All strokes must be applied in the same direction and with the same end of the magnet. After several dozen strokes, retest the nail's magnetism. Does the compass needle move?

The Science
The iron nail is made of a material that can be magnetized. Before being stroked by a magnet, the nail's atoms have magnetic fields that point in all directions, which cancel each other out.

As the nail is stroked, its atomic fields are influenced by the field of the bar magnet. The atoms "feel" the magnetic field and begin to "point" in a common direction. Eventually enough fields "pull together" to produce detectable magnetic properties.

CHECK IT OUT! Design an experiment that would test how back-and-forth strokes induce magnetism.

3.6 UNMAKING A MAGNET

gnikniht ruoy esrever ouy naC
If so, how can you strip a nail of its magnetic properties?

HINT
When the magnetic fields of atoms align, magnetism is produced.
Therefore, when...

Materials

* two magnetized nails
* hammer
* candle
* barbecue tongs
* match
* magnetic compass
* safety goggles

CAUTION
Use the candle only under adult supervision. Before lighting it, make sure that all hair, loose clothing, and hanging jewelry are tied back. Wear safety goggles when striking the nail.

To Do

First use the magnetic compass to test the magnetic properties of the two nails. Observe how far the attraction between each of the nails and the compass needle extends.

Place one of the nails on a vise or shop bench. Put on a pair of safety goggles. Use the hammer to bang the nail several times. Retest the nail's magnetism. Is the nail still magnetic? Has it lost any of its magnetic force?

Now carefully light the candle. Have an adult use barbecue tongs to pick up the second nail and hold it in the flame of the candle for several minutes. Let the nail cool (remember, it's *hot*). Retest the second nail's magnetic strength. Is the nail still magnetic? How far does its field now extend?

The Science

Magnetism depends upon the direction of each atom's magnetic poles (or opposite ends). When the poles of many atoms align, the whole object takes on magnetic properties. By striking the nail with the hammer, you produce tiny changes in the position of its atoms. Although the changes are small, they are enough to affect the direction of the magnetic field. Since fewer fields point in the same direction, the nail loses some of its magnetism.

Heat can also destroy magnetism. As the nail heats up, it expands. This expansion changes the position of the particles and makes them more energetic. These changes shift the direction of the tiny magnetic fields, which decreases the nail's magnetism.

CHECK IT OUT! Design an experiment that would uncover the effects of low temperatures on magnets.

3.7 SHAKE IT UP, BABY!

In our previous experiment, we proved that hammering definitely shakes things up! It pushes some of the atoms this way, others that way. The atomic jumble ruins the magnetic pattern by producing random field directions that cancel each other out.

But you don't need a hammer to shake things up. A simple back-and-forth shake gets the same results.

Materials
* iron filings
* compass
* magnet
* a small plastic vial

To Do

Fill a small vial with iron filings. Gently circle the vial with a compass. Does the compass needle react to the filings?

Hold the vial still. Stroke a strong magnet down the side of the vial in the same direction. (Remember: Back-and-forth movements will undo the magnetic fields that they produce.)

After several dozen strokes, circle the vial once more with the compass. Does the needle now react to the filings? Can you guess what happened?

Put a cap on the vial and shake up the filings. Once more, try the compass test. What happens now? Can you explain what you see (or don't see)?

The Science

At first, the filings were not magnetized. However, after the magnet stroked the vial, the filings took on magnetic properties. The filings' field was strong enough to be detected by the compass. When the vial's contents were shaken, the individual filings moved, shifted, and rotated. At an atomic level, their tiny magnetic fields were no longer aligned. This field hodgepodge canceled itself out and, as a result, the filings lost their magnetic properties.

3.8 POLAR JOURNEY

*H*ave you ever met someone who is your complete opposite? You're sloppy and they're neat. You're loud and they're quiet. You're into science, they HATE it. Opposites, ugh!

But what about magnets? Are they also repelled by opposites, or is there something more, something almost *attractive* about being different?

Materials

* 1-foot long thread
* two clothes pins
* plastic foam "peanuts"
* bar magnet

To Do

Stroke the magnet along the length of one pin. All strokes must be applied in the same direction (from the head end to the point end) and with the same pole of the magnet. After several dozen strokes, the pin should be magnetized. Magnetize a second pin in the same manner.

Insert one of the magnetized pins into a small piece of foam peanut. Gently tie a 1-foot long thread around the peanut so that the pin balances. Tape the free end of the string to the edge of a desk. The pin/foam should hang freely.

Bring the head of the unattached second pin close to the head of the hanging pin. What happens? Try bringing the points of both pins together. What happens now? Now try bringing a head and a point together.

The Science

Each pin has two poles—a north pole and a south pole. Since both pins were magnetized in the same way, their heads were magnetized with the same pole. Likewise, each point took on the same magnetic pole. When the pin heads were brought together, they repelled because charges that are the same repel one another. Likewise, the two points on the pins also repelled. In contrast, when the point and head were brought together, they attracted each other because unlike poles attract.

CHECK IT OUT! Using a compass, how could you identify the pole at the head and point of the pin?

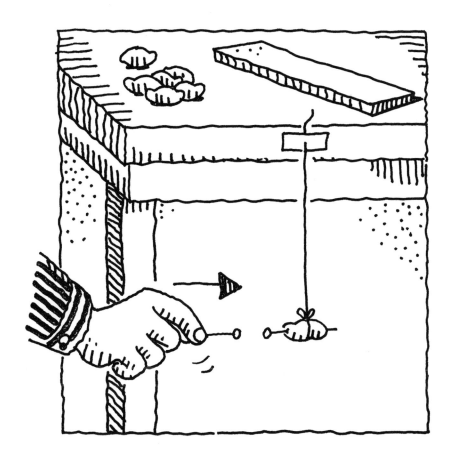

3.9 POLES VERSUS MIDDLE

say it's the poles."

"Well, I say it's the middle."

"Poles."

"Middle."

"POLES!!!"

"MIDDLE!!"

Why not perform a test that will show which (if either) part of the magnet is stronger? That's what a scientist might do!

Materials

* bar magnet
* a bunch of metal paper clips

To Do

Hold the bar magnet by one of its ends. Now bring the other end of the magnet (a pole) in contact with one paper clip. Lift the clip into the air.

Slip together the loops of two paper clips so that a chain of two clips is formed. Now try lifting the chain with the opposite end of the magnet. Keep increasing the number of clips in the chain until you've reach the longest chain that can be picked up by the magnet's pole.

Make a prediction. Will the other pole of the magnet pick up more, fewer, or the same number of clips? Explain your thinking.

Now touch the center of the magnet (between the poles) to a paper clip. Try lifting the clip into the air. What happens? How does the magnetic strength at the center of the magnet compare with the magnetic strength of the poles?

The Science

As you've just discovered, the poles of the magnet have the stronger force. If you were to "see" the magnetic force field, you'd find the lines of force concentrated equally at each pole. This balance results in the equal strength of the north and south pole. There are much fewer magnetic lines of force near the magnet's middle. This results in a much smaller attraction. Clips that are placed here will either drop from the magnet or slide over to the stronger pole regions.

THINK ABOUT IT Why does the shape of a horseshoe result in a magnet's greater lifting capacity?

3.10 CHAIN GAME

Every horror movie buff knows that when a person gets bitten by a vampire, he or she will soon transform into one of the undead. People who are then bitten by this new vampire will also become vampires. It's a deadly chain. From bite to bite, victim to victim, the existence of vampires continues.

Materials
* *bar magnet*
* *dish*
* *a handful of small iron washers*

To Do
Fill a dish with small iron washers. Gently lay the magnet onto this pile. Slowly pick up the magnet. What do you see? Do the washers form a hanging bridge? What part of the magnet do they stick to? Can you explain why the washers behave as they do?

The Science
A magnetic force can travel "through" magnetic objects. The poles are the strongest regions of the magnet. The magnetic force "flows" from these poles to the washers that are in physical contact with the magnet. Those washers now become magnetized and they act as magnets. Any washers in contact with these magnetized washers also become magnetized so that washers in contact with these washers become magnetized. Finally, the magnetized links from both ends of the magnet meet up and form a hanging chain.

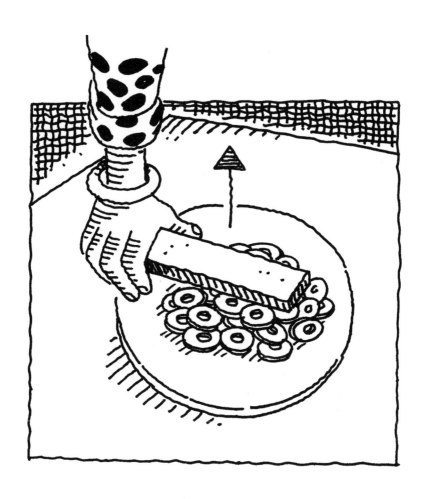

3.11 NORTH-SEEKING NEEDLES

wo thousand years ago, Chinese navigators figured out how magnets could be used in navigation. Some people believe this connection was discovered when someone dropped a piece of natural magnetic rock (called lodestone) into a bucket of water. The rock settled so that it "pointed" to north. Every time it was dropped, the rock came to rest in the same direction.

Materials
* sewing needle
* magnet
* plastic foam cup
* pair of scissors
* a bowl half filled with water

To Do
Carefully remove the circular bottom of a plastic foam cup and place the bottom on the surface of the water. Observe how it floats.

Stroke the magnet along the side of a needle. Remember to stroke only in one direction. Place the magnetized needle on the floating foam bottom.

What happens to the needle and foam?

Now place the magnet along the edge of the bowl. Move the magnet around the bowl. Now what happens to the needle?

The Science
Earth has a magnetic field. Magnetic objects placed within this field will react to this attractive force. When the magnetized needle was placed onto the floating foam, it spun freely. Under the influence of Earth's field, the needle (and float) rotated to its most stable position. Its north-seeking end pointed to the magnetic North Pole.

CHECK IT OUT! A compass on a large ocean vessel is usually located between two spheres. Use a book to find out what these spheres do.

3.12 ATTRACTIVE SHAPES

Water has a skin-like covering formed by the way water molecules attract each other. This attraction is called *surface tension*. Objects such as needles and pins float effortlessly on this invisible skin. Needles and pins are also easily magnetized. Oh? Perhaps we can combine these characteristics?

Materials

* a dozen sewing needles or pins
* magnet
* non-metal bowl
* water
* metal paper clip

To Do

Magnetize about a dozen needles by stroking a permanent magnet along their length. Remember to stroke in only one direction.

Fill a bowl three-fourths full with water. Put a bend in a paper clip, forming a right angle between its two loops. Use this paper clip as a "cradle" to lower needles onto the surface of the water.

Place several needles on the water's surface. Observe how their ends react to each other. What causes some of the needles to attract and others to repel?

Take a look at the shapes shown here. Can you steer the needles into the patterns below? Good luck.

CAUTION

Needles and pins have sharp points. Be careful when handling them. Make sure that when you are finished using these or any other sharp objects all of them are accounted for (and none left in the bowl).

The Science

There are two major concepts at work here. The first is surface tension, which is formed from attractive forces between neighboring water molecules. The second concept is magnetism. As you have learned, like poles repel, while unlike poles attract. In order for needles to align end-to-end, the adjoining ends must have opposite charges. Once they are positioned correctly, the magnetic force helps keep their shape.

CHECK IT OUT! Can you build a magnetic "raft" that can support the weight of an extra large paper clip?

3.13 ANTI-GRAVITY DISKS

Anti-gravity disks? You're kidding.

Yes, we are. But the title probably *did* get your attention. These disks appear to float in mid-air. Their secret isn't an anti-gravity formula handed down by aliens from Mars. It's just a result of magnetic repulsion.

Materials

* four magnets with holes in their center (available at local electronics stores)
* 6-inch-long wooden dowel
* flat wooden base
* carpenter's wood glue

To Do

Cut a piece of ¼-inch wooden dowel about 6 inches long. Make sure that both ends are flat and smooth. Obtain a flat wooden base. Position the dowel in the middle of the base. Secure it to the base with a bead of glue. Let it dry.

Slip a magnet over the dowel. Slip another one on top. If the magnets attract, remove the upper magnet. Flip it upside down so it is repelled by the magnet below. This will make the upper magnet appear to float and bounce in air. Add several more magnets. Make sure that each magnet repels the magnets on either side of it.

The Science

As you've learned, like poles repel and unlike poles attract. We create a force of repulsion by positioning like poles to like poles. This force is strong enough to keep the upper magnets suspended in air.

CHECK IT OUT! Could you keep adding magnets without ever having like poles come in contact? Give it a try!

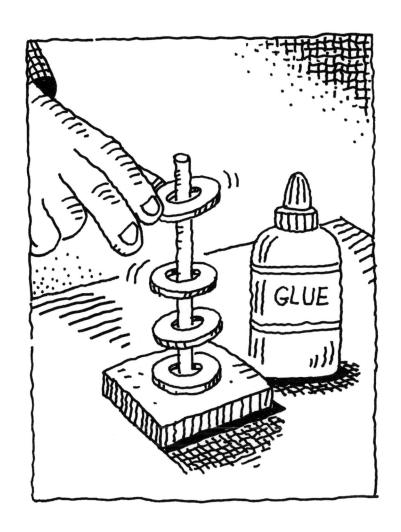

3.14 LIVELY DRAWING

*H*ave you ever wanted to create something that blended art and science? Well, here's your chance! In this experiment, you'll get to construct a drawing that has moving parts. The parts, however, aren't magical—just magnetic.

Materials

* two poster boards or stiff cardboards
* box of crayons
* markers
* tape
* a bunch of metal paper clips
* pair of scissors
* a small magnet

To Do

Draw a colorful setting on a poster board. Be creative. The setting can range from a city street to a fish tank.

Identify several objects that will move around within the setting, such as helicopters, cars, or tropical fishes. Draw these objects on a separate sheet of poster board. Use a pair of scissors to carefully cut out their outlines. Color the objects. Tape a paper clip on the underside of each cutout.

Brace the poster board upright. Position a movable cutout on the scene. Place a magnet behind the board so that it is opposite the object's paper clip. As you move the unseen magnet, the object will move within your scene. What happens to the object when you release the magnet? What happens to the object when you remove the magnet from the back of the board?

The Science

Magnetic fields can easily pass through paper. When the magnet was placed behind the poster board, it attracted the paper clip. The force was so strong that the clip remained held against the upright surface.

CHECK IT OUT! Create an animated story using your setting and characters. Videotape it and show it to your friends.

3.15 IRON-FILLED BREAKFAST

*I*ron is a nutrient that is essential for maintaining good health. It helps form a chemical within the blood called hemoglobin, which is found in red blood cells. There, it transports oxygen from the lungs to every cell in the body. Without iron, we couldn't make hemoglobin and our cells would die from lack of oxygen.

Materials
* iron-enriched cereal
* strong magnet
* a white piece of paper
* plastic bag
* a spoon

To Do
Place a spoonful of iron-enriched cereal into a small plastic bag. Use the back end of a spoon to crush the cereal grains. Keep crushing them until all the grains are made into a fine powder.

Carefully pour out the powder onto a sheet of clean, white paper. Place a strong magnet below the paper. Slowly move the magnet back-and-forth. What do you observe?

The Science
Iron-enriched cereal contains the element iron. The iron is bound up into the cereal grains. When the grains are crushed, the small fragments containing iron are produced. These fragments are "light" enough to respond to magnetic fields. The cereal dust on the paper "dances" to the movement of the magnet below.

CHECK IT OUT! Crush the contents of a daily vitamin pill that is iron-enriched. Can you observe any evidence of iron in the pill's contents?

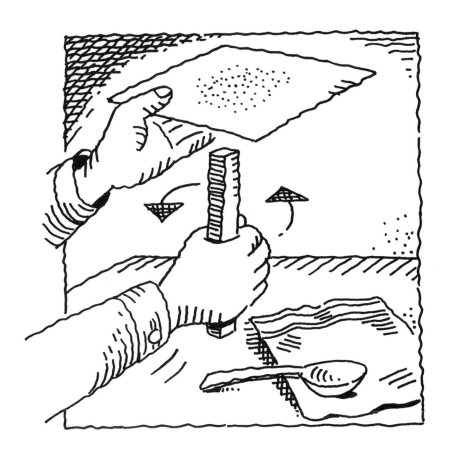

3.16 MAGNETIC MUSCLE

*T*his one is stronger."
"No, this one is stronger."
"I say it's this one!"
"Well, I insist it's this one!"
"This one!!"
"THIS ONE!!!"
Why not test both of the magnets and compare?

Materials

* * a bunch of metal paper clips
* * 1-foot-long string
* * wooden or plastic ruler
* * stack of books
* * a variety of magnets

To Do

Cut a length of string about 1 foot long. Tie one end of the string to a magnet. Tape the other end to the end of a ruler. Position the ruler so that the magnet extends beyond the edge of the desk. Secure the ruler with a small stack of books.

Place a paper clip in your palm. Raise the clip so that it touches the pole of the hanging magnet. Gently lower your hand. Is the magnet strong enough to hold up the clip?

Slip together the loops of two paper clips so that a chain of two clips is formed. Repeat the magnet test. Can the magnet support two clips? Next, try three. Keep going until you reach the limit that can be supported by this magnet.

The Science

Magnets vary in strength. You can create a scale of relative strength by comparing how many paper clips each magnet can support.

Over time, magnets lose some of their power. The magnetic fields of individual atoms start "pointing" in different directions. As more atoms begin to point randomly, the magnet loses its strength.

CHECK IT OUT! Do you wear an electronic wristwatch? If so, you should be careful when handling powerful magnets. Some magnets can produce a magnetic field that is strong enough to ruin watches and other electronic devices.

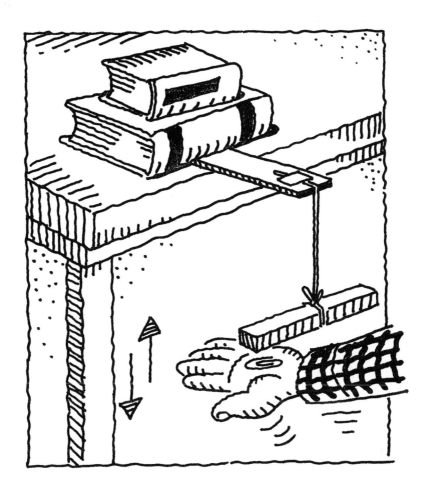

3.17 MAGNETIC EXTENSION

Suppose a paper clip is placed against the north pole of a strong magnet. Does the end of the clip that is in contact with the magnet also become a north pole? If so, will the entire clip be a "northern extension" of the magnet and lack any sort of south pole? Or will the whole clip become a south pole and lack any northern identity? Maybe it will have both a north and south pole? Maybe neither? Make a guess and then explore the nature of the clip's poles.

Materials
* *metal paper clip*
* *bar magnet*
* *compass*

To Do
Place the north end of a magnet near a compass. Observe and record which end of the compass needle points to the magnet. Now place a paper clip on the magnet's north end. The clip should be positioned so that it extends straight out from the magnet, maintaining the magnet's straight line appearance.

Move the compass near the free end of the magnetized clip. Which end of the compass points to the free end of the clip? Can you explain what you see? Suppose the compass is brought near the contact point of the clip and magnet. In which direction will it point?

The Science
When a clip is placed in contact with the magnet, magnetism is induced in the clip. The clip "lengthens" the magnet by extending the pole farther out.

CHECK IT OUT! Although magnets can have more than two poles, there are no known magnets that have only a single pole. All magnets must have at least one north pole and one south pole.

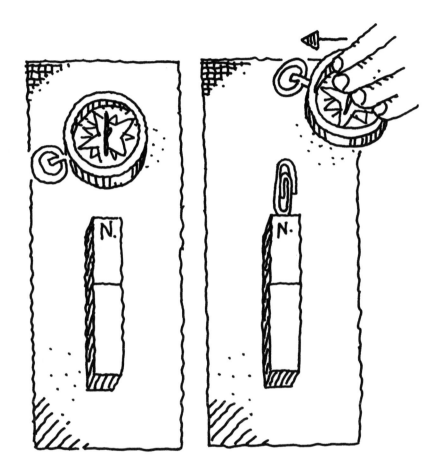

3.18 FLYING SAUCER WITH CUP

Do you like to confuse people? If so, this next experiment may be just the thing. It's an impossible sight that's made possible by a magnet's invisible force field.

Materials
* *paper*
* *markers or crayons*
* *metal paper clip*
* *10-inch-long string*
* *tape*
* *strong and flat magnet*
* *stack of books*
* *a pair of scissors*

To Do
Draw and color a small picture of a coffee cup sitting on top of a saucer. Cut out this object. Use tape to secure the back of this picture to a metal paper clip.

Cut a length of string about 10 inches long. Tie one end of the string to the paper clip. Tape the other end of the string to a desk.

Hide a flat magnet between the pages of a book. Place this book atop a stack of other books. Position the stack so that the picture is attracted to the magnet. When raised, the cup and saucer should float in mid-air with no apparent reason for the gravity-defying behavior.

The Science
Although it isn't visible, the magnetic field exists. The hidden magnet's attraction is strong enough to overcome the weight of the clip, paper, tape, and string.

CHECK IT OUT! Suppose the paper clip was replaced by another magnet. How would this change the effect?

3.19 FIELD BLOCKERS

*N*ow that you've had some experience with magnetic fields, it's time to make some predictions. Examine the list below and circle the materials that you believe will block a magnetic field.

* aluminum foil
* wood
* piece of videocassette tape

* audio CD
* turntable record
* coins

Now test out your predictions by doing the following experiment.

Materials
* *metal paper clip*
* *10-inch-long string*
* *tape*
* *strong magnet*

* *wooden or plastic ruler*
* *stack of books*
* *the materials listed above*

To Do

Cut a length of string about 10 inches long. Tie one end of the string to the paper clip. Tape the other end of the string to a desk.

Tape a magnet to the end of a ruler. Insert the ruler between the pages of a book so that the magnet is extended as far from the book as possible. Place this book on top of a stack of several books.

Position the stack so that the magnet is positioned directly above the paper clip. The clip's string should be short enough to create a gap between the clip and magnet, but long enough for the clip to remain supported by the magnet's attraction.

Place various objects directly between the magnet and the clip. Record how the magnetic field behaves.

The Science

Some materials (those made of iron) will block a magnetic field. Most materials, however, do not and will allow the penetration of the field.

CHECK IT OUT! Can you magnetize a length of videotape that has been removed from a discarded cassette?

3.20 AUTO-MOTION

*H*ere's another one of those *just-for-fun* experiments.

Materials
- *foam core board*
- *markers*
- *a pair of chopsticks*
- *two magnets*
- *stiff paper*
- *a bunch of metal paper clips*
- *tape*
- *four books of the same width*

To Do
Sketch a bird's-eye view of a roadway onto a large piece of foam core board. The road should split, connect, and form several intersections. Include things like houses, factories, rivers, and garages along the road. Elevate the board by supporting each corner with a book.

Copy the car shown below onto a piece of stiff paper. You may wish to make other vehicles, such as fire engines, ambulances, and construction trucks. Bend the paper along the dotted line. Tape a paper clip to the upper surface of the lower fold (see illustration). Put the car on the roadway of the foam core board.

Tape a magnet to the end of a chopstick. Place the end of the stick with the magnet under the foam core board where the car is. As you move the stick, the magnet and car should move along the roadway.

The Science

Foam core does not interfere with magnetic fields. Magnets placed below the roads attracted the paper clip vehicles. As the magnets moved, they dragged the clips (along with their attached vehicles) across the foam core's surface.

CHECK IT OUT! Try building a magnetic airport or harbor.

3.21 SEPARATION ANXIETY

*O*kay, who did it? Who mixed the iron filings with the salt? Anyone have any bright ideas about how to separate these two substances?

Materials
* sealable plastic bag
* magnet
* 1 teaspoon salt
* plate
* ¼ teaspoon iron filings

To Do
Add about ¼ teaspoon of iron filings to 1 teaspoon of salt. Mix well and pour this blend onto a plate.

Seal the magnet in the plastic bag. Predict what will happen when you move the magnet through the mixture. After you make your prediction, find out what happens.

The Science
The iron filings are attracted to the magnet and stick to the bag's outer surface. The salt (which isn't a magnetic material) remains behind.

Another Solution
Add the salt-and-iron mixture to a large container of warm (not hot) water. Stir vigorously. The salt crystals will dissolve into the water by breaking down into invisible atom-sized particles. These particles mix so thoroughly in water that they won't sink or accumulate at the bottom. This type of mixture is called a *solution*.

In contrast, iron doesn't dissolve in water. Its particles remain their filing size. In water, the filings fall and accumulate at the bottom of the container.

If this solution is poured through filter paper, the dissolved salt flows with the water. The iron filings, however, will get trapped by the paper.

INDEX

ANSWERS TO CHECK IT OUT!

p. 9 corners of an equilateral triangle; p. 10 yes; p. 12 yes; p. 14 yes; p. 22 too heavy; p. 26 induction of charge; p. 28 yes; p. 36 winter/drier; p. 38 prevent sparks; p. 40 many including glass/silk, rubber/fur; p. 42 observe attraction/repulsion to positive nylon; p. 44 inquiry based upon ability of TV to broadcast spark cracks; p. 46 difficult—too similar in weight; p. 48 insulator material would not ground out charge; p. 51 dice tossed by Lucite attraction; p. 52 thickness increases thread weight; p. 55 yes; p. 59 depends upon charging procedure; p. 63 replace aluminum with thin plastic; p. 64 yes; p. 103 yes, replacement produces less current; p. 118 similar-looking force lines that connect side-by-side poles; p. 125 compare and contrast magnets made with one-way to back-and-forth strokes; p. 127 measure magnetic strength of magnets placed in freezer; p. 140 no—weight would eventually press bottom magnets together; p. 131 analyze attraction/repulsion behavior; p. 133 two side-by-side poles pull together; p. 136 filter out the unwanted magnetic fields; p. 150 greater space between magnets; p. 152 yes

ABOUT THE AUTHOR

MICHAEL ANTHONY DISPEZIO is a renaissance educator who teaches, writes, and conducts teacher workshops throughout the world. He received an M.A. in biology from Boston University, and for six summers was a research assistant to Nobel laureate Albert Szent-Gyorgyi.

After tiring of counting hairs on copepods, Michael traded the marine science laboratory for the classroom. Over the years, he has taught physics, chemistry, earth science, general science, mathematics, and rock 'n' roll musical theater.

To date, Michael is the author of *Critical Thinking Puzzles, Great Critical Thinking Puzzles, Challenging Critical Thinking Puzzles,* and *Visual Thinking Puzzles* (all from Sterling). He is also the co-author of eighteen elementary, middle, and high school science textbooks and has been a "hired creative-gun" for clients including The Weather Channel and Children's Television Workshop. He also develops activities for the classroom guides to *Discover* magazine and *Scientific American Frontiers.*

Michael was a contributor to the National Science Teachers Association's Pathways to Science Standards. This document set offers guidelines for moving the national science standards from vision to practice. Michael's work with the NSTA has also included authoring the critically acclaimed NSTA curriculum, *The Science of HIV.*